ALGORITHMS

PRACTICAL GUIDE TO LEARN
ALGORITHMS FOR BEGINNERS

Andy Vickler

Table of Contents

Introduction

If you want to step into the world of programming and coding, you must understand the basics. You cannot develop complex programs or products with limited knowledge of programming. At the base of every computer program is an algorithm. If you want to write efficient and effective code, you must write algorithms first, and to do this, you must understand what an algorithm is. This is the only way you can develop the right program.

If you are unsure of what an algorithm is or want to learn the basics again, you are in the right place. This book has all the information you need to understand algorithms and how they can be used to develop good code or programs. You must develop the right algorithm, especially if you want to write the perfect code. An algorithm is a set of rules or instructions, which indicate to a machine or computer the process it should follow to achieve the result.

Throughout the book, you will learn about the different types of algorithms and how they can be used to solve a variety of problems. The book also introduces you to some programming concepts, and you need to understand these concepts to ensure you develop the right code once you have an algorithm in place. Since algorithms form the base for any code you write, it is also important to include certain statements to handle different types of errors. You will learn how to do this and what lines of code to include to handle errors in the code.

The book covers some of the most common algorithms, including search, sort, loops, decision-making statements, and more. It also includes some examples and programs which will make it easier for you to convert an algorithm into a program when you need to. It is important to understand that you cannot become an expert at coding if you do not understand the basics. Therefore, use the information in the book to help you improve your understanding of coding and practice as often as you can so you master writing algorithms and programs.

Thank you for purchasing the book. I hope the book covers all the information you are looking for.

Chapter One

Introduction to Algorithms

A programmer needs to know what an algorithm is, so they know how to use it to write code. An algorithm is a set of rules, instructions, or processes any machine or system should follow to solve a problem. It can include the type of operations to use and the variables one should declare. In simple words, an algorithm is a set of rules defining the steps to complete to obtain the desired results.

Any recipe you follow is an algorithm. If you want to try a new dish, you read the instructions or steps given. Only when you do this can you make the perfect dish. It is also important to follow the instructions to the tee. An algorithm ensures a system performs a task, so the user obtains the expected output. Algorithms are very simple instructions, and you can implement one in any programming language as long as you understand the syntax. The output will be the same.

Association between Algorithms and Computer Science

If you want the computer to complete any task, you must write a program. Using this program, you can tell the computer exactly what it needs to do, so you receive the required output. Ensure the steps are defined clearly. The computer will follow these steps and will accomplish the end result. Ensure you choose the right input variables and information to feed the computer so you obtain the right output. Algorithms are the best way to get a task done.

Characteristics of an Algorithm

Let us continue with the example of a recipe. If you want to prepare something new, you need to follow numerous instructions. You will do your best to stick to the recipe, but you may improvise if you do not have a specific ingredient. In the same way, you cannot convert a program into an algorithm since not every statement is a part of an algorithm. Regardless of how you write an algorithm, it will have the following characteristics:

Feasible

Algorithms should be simple, generic, and practical. Ensure any programming language can execute this algorithm based on the resources the programming language has available. Do not write an algorithm without knowing how to use a programming language to code it. Instead, it must be written based on the relevant information about its use.

Finite

Any algorithm you write should be finite. If you use loops or any other function, ensure the algorithm ends. Do not have an infinite or circular reference that can leave the algorithm running continuously.

No Dependence on Language

No algorithm should have a dependency on a programming language. The instructions should be precise and simple. Ensure you can use any programming language to write your algorithm. As mentioned earlier, the output will be the same.

Unambiguity

Every algorithm you write should be clear and unambiguous. Every step should be clear and should only mean one thing. The compiler should never be given a chance to think of two or three different ways to perform a certain step. Every instruction must be clear in every aspect.

Well-Defined Inputs

When you make a new dish, you should look at the relevant ingredients and ensure they are exactly what you need to make the dish. This is the same for the inputs you enter when writing an algorithm.

Well-Defined Outputs

If you follow the instructions given in a recipe to the tee, your dish will be exactly what you decided to make. Ensure that the algorithm you write will clearly define the type of output you want to obtain. This means you must define the output clearly, as well.

Designing an Algorithm

Before you write any algorithm, ask yourself the following questions:

- What inputs do you want to use for the algorithm?

- What constraints must you bear in mind when you try to solve this problem?

- What is the desired or expected output?

- What problem are you trying to solve by writing this algorithm?

- What is the solution to the problem based on the constraints?

These questions make it easier for you to generate the correct output. It helps you think clearly, so you write an effective algorithm. Let us look at an example now where we are trying to multiply three numbers and print the product of those numbers.

Step One: Identifying the Problem Statement

It is important to answer the questions above before writing an algorithm. Let us assume we want to write an algorithm to multiply three numbers and calculate the output. Therefore, the problem statement here is to calculate the product of three numbers.

Once you do this, you must identify the desired output, constraints, desired inputs, and the solution to the problem. One of the constraints you must add is to ensure the user enters only numbers to calculate the product. This means your input needs to be three numbers, and its output should be the product of those three numbers. The solution is to use the multiplication operator '*' to calculate the product of the numbers entered as the input.

Step Two: Designing the Algorithm

The next thing to do is to design the algorithm using the information you identified in the above step.

1. Begin the algorithm

2. Declare and initialize the variables as y and z

3. Now, assign values to these variables. Ensure you assign the first value to x, second value to y, and third value to z

4. Declare and initialize the output variable to store the product of the input variables

5. Now, multiply the variables and store the product in the output variable declared in the previous step

6. Print the output value

7. End the algorithm

Step Three: Test the Algorithm

Now, use any programming language to write this algorithm and test the function of the algorithm.

How to Identify the Best Algorithm

You can choose an algorithm based on the following criteria:

- Accuracy of the algorithm to ensure that you obtain the expected result regardless of the number of times you use the algorithm. An incorrect algorithm will either give you an incorrect output or may not use all input instances

- Identify the different constraints you need to consider when developing the algorithm

- Define the efficiency of the algorithm based on the order of inputs you will use to obtain the expected output

- Assess and understand the computer architecture and the devices used to run the algorithm

Understanding the Basic Algorithm that Digitally Powers Life

Algorithms instruct the machine to perform a set of instructions to obtain the solution. These algorithms are the basis of all technology. The algorithm can be used to solve any type of problem, including compressing a file, determining the pages on the internet that have the most relevance to your search or sorting a list. An algorithm can be used to determine the way a traffic signal should work, how the postal services or any other courier service can deliver mail, and more.

In this day and age, a child needs to learn more than just how to use technology. They must explore different algorithms that power the television at home or their phones. They should also learn more about the algorithms used on different social media websites. This will help them improve their programming skills and work on creating new technology.

Benefits of Algorithmic Thinking

It is extremely important to learn more about algorithms, especially when writing code to solve difficult mathematical and scientific problems. You can solve any scientific or mathematical problem if you think clearly. This type of thinking is known as algorithmic thinking. You may have used algorithmic thinking to solve many problems. For example, when you try to add two numbers, you think about the first number's value and the second number's value. You then think about where to store the sum of the two numbers and how to add those numbers. This is a very simple example of algorithmic thinking.

Another example can be to solve a long division problem. You apply the algorithm to divide every digit in the number with a divisor. For every digit in the number being divided, you should multiply, subtract and divide. It becomes easier to break a problem into smaller problems through algorithmic thinking. You also look for solutions based on the type of problem you are looking at.

Coding is an art, and it is important to learn how to do this since it improves your thinking capabilities. Look at different exercises and puzzles that can help to improve your way of thinking. Choose those exercises and puzzles that give you a better understanding of conditional logic, sequencing, and repetition.

You Can Write Your Own Algorithm

If you have long morning routines, you can choose to create a simpler task for yourself. Set small targets for yourself in the algorithm and forget about any overhead tasks you may have to perform. You will soon learn about some important concepts of algorithms, such as repetition (brush the bottom row of teeth four times), sequencing (putting the cereal in a bowl and then pouring milk), and conditional logic (do not eat if the bowl is empty).

If you want to improve in writing algorithms, add a few more challenges to yourself. A computer does not understand the intentions behind your instructions unless you explicitly mention them. For example, you will teach your child to add milk to the bowl of cereal only after placing the bowl of milk in front of him. If you do not do this, the milk will be all over the table. The same is the case with machines – if your instructions are not clear, you will never get the required result.

In your arithmetic class, you will have learned about prime numbers and how to determine if a number is prime. Can you do this with a number like 123459734? You cannot unless you perform multiple calculations. It does become easier to run a program to do this for you, but the code will only work if your algorithm is right.

Pros and Cons

Most programmers use algorithms to design their approach to any problem before writing the code. An algorithm does have its advantages, but there are many disadvantages to using algorithms. This section will look at some of the pros and cons of algorithms.

Pros

1. Algorithms allow you to divide or break the problem into a smaller segment, and this makes it easier for a developer or programmer to write this algorithm in the form of a program depending on the type of programming language you want to use

2. The procedure is precise and definite

3. An algorithm is a step-by-step representation of the solution for any problem. This means that it is easy for anybody to understand an algorithm

4. It is easy to understand an algorithm, and therefore, it becomes easier for you to identify any errors in the code based on the algorithm you have written

5. As mentioned earlier, algorithms are not dependent on the type of programming language used. This means that they are easy for anybody to understand even if they have no knowledge of programming.

Cons

1. You cannot use an algorithm to explain or depict a large program

2. Since algorithms are not computer programs, you need to put in extra effort to develop a computer program

3. It will take a long time to write complex algorithms

Chapter Two

Types of Algorithms

This chapter will look at some types of algorithms and how they can be used while you write code. The types of algorithms include:

1. Backtracking algorithm

2. Brute Force algorithm

3. Divide and conquer algorithm

4. Dynamic programming algorithm

5. Greedy algorithm

6. Randomized algorithm

7. Simple recursive algorithm

Backtracking Algorithm

A backtracking algorithm is not very easy to use, but you can write a program easily if you understand the concept. Let us understand this algorithm using the following example. Consider we have one problem. Now, you divide this problem into six smaller problems.

Try solving the smaller problems first. It may seem like these smaller solutions will not solve the larger problem. So, what should I do in this case?

Look at the subproblems to identify which subproblem the main problem depends on. Once you do this, you can identify the solution to the larger problem. The objective behind this algorithm is to look at the problem from the start if you cannot solve the main problem. When you start off with the first subproblem and cannot find a solution, backtrack and go to the beginning. Try to find a solution to the problem.

A classic example of this algorithm is the N Queens problem. In this problem, you should find a way to add the maximum number of queens on a chessboard and ensure no queen can attack the other on this board. If you want to understand this easier, let us look at this example using four queens.

If you use four queens, your output will be a binary matrix. It will represent the queen's position on the chessboard. Let us represent the position using 1s. The output matrix could be as follows for 4 queens:

```
{ 0,   0,   0,   1}
{ 0,   0,   1,   0}
{ 0,   1,   0,   0}
{ 1,   0,   0,   0}
```

The objective of this problem is to place a queen in different columns. Based on the output, you know that you should start with the leftmost column on the chessboard. When you place the queen in a column, you must check if the position will clash with other queens on the board. If you find a position that does not clash with the position of the other queens, you can mark that row and column as the solution. If you cannot find the right position, you should go back to the start and begin again.

You can write the algorithm in the following manner:

1. Place the queen on the leftmost column of your chessboard

2. If you can place queens on the chessboard in such a way that no two queens can attack each other, return the value as true

3. You must check and try every row in the chessboard and perform the following activities:

   a. If you place a queen in one row and ensure there are no clashes between the queens on the board, write the row and column number in a solution matrix. Using this matrix, see if you can find a solution

   b. If you place a queen in the position where you receive a solution, you can return the algorithm as true

   c. Else, you should remove the row and column number from the solution matrix and find a new combination

4. If you have tried all the rows and nothing works, then return false and move back to the first step.

Brute Force Algorithm

If you use this algorithm, you must look at every possible solution until you find the optimal solution to any problem. This type of algorithm will be used to find the best solution once it checks all the optimal solutions for a problem. If you find a solution to the problem, you can stop the algorithm at that moment and find the solution to this problem. A classic example of this algorithm is the exact string-matching algorithm, where you try to match a string in a text.

Divide and Conquer Algorithm

As the name suggests, the divide and conquer algorithm divides the problem into numerous segments. You then need to use a recursive function to solve these subproblems and combine the solutions obtained to form the solution of the main problem. Merge and quick sort algorithms are examples of this divide and conquer algorithm. We will look at these examples in detail later in the book.

Using the divide and conquer algorithmic approach gives you a chance to solve multiple subproblems at the same time using parallelism. You can do this since the subproblems are independent. This means any algorithm you develop using the divide and conquer technique can run on different processes and machines at once. These algorithms use recursion, and it is for this reason that memory management is of utmost importance.

Dynamic Programming Algorithm

The dynamic programming algorithm, also called a dynamic optimization algorithm, uses the past information to define the new solution. Using this algorithm makes it easier to break a complex problem into smaller subproblems. It is easier to solve the smaller problems using the algorithm. You can use these results to solve the actual problem. The results of the subproblems are stored in other variables. This reduces the runtime of the algorithm. Consider the following example of a pseudocode used to give the Fibonacci series as the output.

```
Fibonacci (x)
If x = 0
     Return 0
Else
     Previous_Fibonacci =0,
Current_Fibonacci = 1
     Repeat n-1 times
     Next_Fibonacci = Previous_Fibonacci +
Current_Fibonacci
     Previous_Fibonacci = Current_Fibonacci
     Current_Fibonacci = New_Fibonacci
Return Current_Fibonacci
```

In the example above, the base value in the code is set to zero. This problem is divided into different subproblems, and you can store the values or the results of these subproblems into other variables. To do this, use the following approach:

1. Identify the solution to the problem and define the structure of the solution you want to design

2. Use recursion to define the solution

3. Solve for the value of the solution using the bottom-up fashion.

4. Using the results or information from the computation, develop the optimal solution

Greedy Algorithm

Using the greedy algorithm, it becomes easier to divide the problem into smaller problems and find the right solution to these subproblems. It will then try to find the optimal solution for the main problem. Having said that, do not expect to find the optimal solution to a problem using this algorithm. Some examples of this algorithm are the Huffman coding problem and counting money.

Let us consider the former example. In the Huffman coding problem, you try to compress data without losing any information from the set you have. This means you must first assign values to different input characters. If you use a programming language to replicate this algorithm, the length of the code will vary depending on how often you use the input characters to solve the problem. Every character you use will have a smaller code, but the code's length depends on how often you use the variable or character. When it comes to solving this problem, you need to consider two parts:

1. Developing and creating the Huffman tree

2. Traversing the tree to find the solution

Consider the string "YYYZXXYYZ." If you count the number of characters in this string, the highest frequency is "Y," and the character with the least frequency is "Z." When you write the code using any programming language, the code will be the smallest for Y and the largest for Z. The complexity of assigning code for these characters is dependent on the frequency of that character.

Let us now look at the input and output variables.

Input: For this example, let us look at a string that has different characters, say "BCCBEBFFFFADCEFLLKLKKEEBFF"

Output: Let us now assign the code for each of these characters:

```
Data: F, Frequency: 7, Code: 01
Data: L, Frequency: 3, Code: 0001
Data: K, Frequency: 3, Code: 0000
Data: C, Frequency: 3, Code: 101
Data: B, Frequency: 4, Code: 100
Data: D, Frequency: 1, Code: 110
Data: E, Frequency: 4, Code: 001
```

Let us now look at how you can write the algorithm to build the tree:

1. Declare and initialize a string that has different characters.

2. Assign codes to each of the characters in the string.

3. Build the Huffman tree.

   a. Define each node in the tree based on the node's character, frequency, and right and left child.

b. Create the frequency list and store the frequency of every character in that list. The frequency should be assigned to zero for the characters.

c. For every character in the string, increase the frequency in the list if it is present.

d. End the loop.

e. If the frequency is non-zero, then add the character to the node of the tree and assign a priority to the node as Q.

4. If the priority list, Q, is not empty, remove the item from the list and assign it to the left node. Else assign it to the right node.

5. Move across the node to find the code assigned to the character.

6. End the algorithm.

If you want to traverse or move across the tree, use the following input:

1. The Huffman tree and the node

2. The code assigned to the node

The output will leave you with the character and the code assigned to that character.

1. If the left child of the node is a null value, then traverse through the right child and assign the code 1

2. If the left child of the node is not a null value, then traverse through that child and assign the code zero

3. Display the characters with their current code

Randomized Algorithm

If you use a randomized algorithm, you use a random number to make decisions. These decisions are used to solve some algorithms. A quick sort algorithm is an example of this type of algorithm, and we will look at this later in the book.

Simple Recursive Algorithm

Using a simple recursive algorithm, you can solve different problems easily. This algorithm is often used along with other algorithms. A simple recursive algorithm recurs using a smaller input value every time it begins. In this type of algorithm, you need to set a base value that will indicate to the system that the algorithm needs to terminate. A simple recursive algorithm is often used to solve any problem as long as it can be divided into smaller pieces or segments. Bear in mind these segments should also be of the same type. Let us look at how you can use this algorithm to calculate the factorial of a number. Consider the following pseudocode:

```
Factorial(number)
If number is 0
     Return 1
Else
     Return (number*Factorial(number - 1)
```

The base value used in the above code is zero. This indicates the algorithm will not continue to work if the output value is zero. If you look at the last section of the algorithm, you will notice the problem is broken down into smaller segments to solve it.

Chapter Three

Describing Algorithms

I t is important to describe algorithms effectively since this is the only way you can solve the problem. In the previous chapter, we looked at different algorithms you should consider and how to use them to solve problems. Most of the types we discussed in the previous chapter broke the problem into smaller segments making it easier to solve the actual problem. Ensure you use the algorithm that works best for you. This algorithm should also require minimal or no changes to the data structures for the program. For example, if you use the bubble sort algorithm, ensure you store the information you need to use in an array or another data structure. You should then use the comparison and exchange operations to update the data. We will look at the bubble sort algorithm in further detail later in the book.

If you want to use data structures, describe the structure well, making it easier to build it. For example, using the merge sort algorithm makes it easier to compare information in the data set faster than the quick sort algorithm. The merge sort algorithm only has some errors when compared to the quick sort algorithm. You will, however, need to use a linked list data structure if you want to sort this information easily. This data structure will improve the performance of the algorithm.

Ensure you include all the necessary information when you use a merge sort algorithm. These instructions should include error checking, error handling, and pointer manipulation. When you describe any algorithm, you need to pay attention to how abstract you want the algorithm to be. It is impossible to describe everything in the algorithm in detail, but you must do this when writing code. You also cannot leave the algorithm in a black box. If you are a good programmer or know someone who will build the right code for you, you can simply say, "Use bubble sort." It is, however, good to explain your algorithm in as much detail as possible.

You must consider the following when you add details about the algorithm you want to use:

- What is the purpose of the algorithm? Is it to perform any functions on the code or information in the data?

- Are there specific data structures you must use to manipulate the information used in the algorithm?

- Mention the steps and add details wherever possible, so anybody reading the algorithm knows what must be done

- Justify the correctness of the algorithm

- Analyze the speed, cost, space, etc. used by the algorithm

It is also important to describe the algorithm depending on the audience and the purpose. If you want to use a new algorithm to solve a well-known problem, emphasize the technique you use, the justification of the correctness, and the analysis of that algorithm. You must show how your algorithm is better than the one used earlier. If you present or use a new data structure, mention why you want to use them and how you plan to analyze the problem using that structure.

Some tools that you use to prove the correctness of the algorithm will enable you to describe the algorithm in a better manner. You should not ignore this entirely.

Chapter Four

Error Handling

As mentioned earlier, it is important to look at how to handle errors in any algorithm and code. It is simple to understand this concept. All you must do is identify lines of code you should write to ensure errors and exceptions are handled. One of the easiest things to do is to use certain keywords, like null, to handle errors and exceptions in your code. It is important to understand that programming languages use the keyword differently. Ensure you have the right error handling code in place, but if the code obscures the logic, then do not include the error handling code in your main code. Here are some tips you must bear in mind:

- You can include the catch keyword in the code to identify errors, but it is important to use the keyword in the right location. You must also use the 'try' keyword to identify the error in the code. Ensure that you start the error handling code with a try-catch-finally statement while you write the code

- If you add an exception to the code, you must provide the compiler with enough information to allow you to determine the position of the error in the code. Create an informative error message and pass that message to the exception. It is also important to ensure the operation you are performing in the code did not work the way it is expected to work

- Instead of pointing the compiler to a block of error code in the program, it is best to throw an exception. If you do not point the compiler to an error code in the program, you must indicate to the compiler to look for the issue in the code and debug it. If you do write the code, make sure you know where you have added this code. Throw exceptions when there is an error in the code to avoid issues with the debugging of the code

Checking for Exceptions

Unfortunately, programming languages do not list different exception and error handling techniques, but you should do your best to see how to use these techniques to handle errors in the code. You must also include these error-handling techniques when you write the algorithm. A checked exception will allow you to ensure that the signature of every function or method used in the code will have the list of every exception that will pass to the caller.

It is important to understand that the compiler will not execute the code if the signature does not match it. In the example below, we will look at how to use exception and error handling codes in Java.

```
public void ioOperation(boolean isResourceAvailable) throws
IOException {

    if (!isResourceAvailable) {
      throw new IOException();
    }
  }
```

An issue with this form of exception is it may violate some rules of programming languages. If you can throw any checked exception using a method in the code and the catch is three lines above the code, declare an exception in the method's signature. This means some blocks of code will change because of the exception handling or error handling blocks of code.

Defining Exceptions

It is of utmost importance to define the exceptions in the code based on the needs of the function. So, how is it that you will classify errors? Will you classify them based on their type so you know whether it is because of a network failure, programming error, or device failure? Will you classify them based on their source so you know where these errors come from? Or will you classify the errors based on how the compiler identifies these errors?

Some programming languages allow you to convert blocks of existing code into exception or error handling code. In the example below, we will see how this can be done:

```
class LocalPort {
  private let innerPort: ACMEPort   func
open() throws {
```

```
    do {
      try innerPort.open()
    } catch let error as DeviceResponseError
{
      throw
PortDeviceFailure.portDeviceFailure(error:
error)
    } catch let error as
ATM1212UnlockedError {
      throw
PortDeviceFailure.portDeviceFailure(error:
error)
    } catch let error as GMXError {
      throw
PortDeviceFailure.portDeviceFailure(error:
error)
    }
  }
}
```

Special Case Patterns

Programming languages also allow you to create or configure an object, so it handles certain types of errors in the code. The client or main code will not deal with any exceptional behavior.

Now that we have looked at the different ways to handle code let us look at the use of the null keyword to handle errors.

Nulls

If you add a null keyword into a method, the code you have written will become impossible to debug. It is important that you avoid doing this. Adding null values to the error handling code increases work for you. If the output is a null value, you must struggle to identify where the null value came up in your code.

```swift
// Un-swifty, but matches code in book
func register(item: Item?) {
  if item != nil {
    let registry: ItemRegistry? =
persitentStore.getItemRegistry()
    if registry != nil {
      let existingItem =
registry.getItem(item.getId())
      if
existingItem.getBillingPeriod().hasRetailOwn
er()) {
        existingItem.register(item)
      }
    }
  }
}// More Swifty using guard statements.
func register(item: Item?) {
  guard let item = item,
        let registry =
persistentStore.getItemRegistry() else {
    return
  }
  let existingItem =
registry.getItem(item.getId())
  guard
existingItem.getBillingPeriod().hasRetailOwn
er() else {
    return
  }
  existingItem.register(item)
}
```

Common Error Messages

Simple programs are easy to compile. You may not have errors in the code if you have stuck to the algorithm and used the right variable to code. This should not make you overconfident since this is usually not the case. As a programmer, you will spend most of your time dealing with certain flaws in the program you have written. The process of fixing the errors is called debugging.]This section will look at different ways to handle errors in any program you have written.

Editing and Recompiling

You may have spelling issues in your code. This may not seem like a big issue, but the compiler will throw an error if you have the wrong words in the code. This indicates you must go through the code to fix the error. Do not worry about dealing with too many errors since this is the only way you learn. You will need to go through the following steps to overcome any errors in your code. You must follow the steps given below to re-run the code.

- Reedit the source code and save the file to the disk

- Recompile the code

- Run the program

You may still have many errors while re-editing your code. Do not worry since you will get to step 3 once you identify how to work with and edit the errors in programs.

Reedit the source code

The source code file you create can be changed as often as possible. More often than not, these changes are necessary to overcome any error messages that come up during compiling. At times, you may want to change the code by changing the message that comes up on the screen or by adding a feature.

Recompile

In this step, you must run the program one more time and compile it once you have made changes to the code. Link the program to the compiler. Since the code is different, you must send the code to the compiler only after you link the code. If the compiler throws an error again, you must repeat the first step again. To recompile the program one more time, enter the following code in the command prompt to trigger the compiler:

```
gcc hello.c -0 hello
```

If no error message pops up, pat yourself on the back. You no longer have errors in your code.

Dealing with errors

When you write code, it is important to understand errors will pop up in the code. Do not worry about these errors, but learn from them to avoid making the same mistakes again. The compiler helps you identify the exact line in the code where there is an error, thereby helping you get rid of it easily. Consider the example below:

```c
#include <stdio.h>
int main()
{
printf("This program will err.\n")
return(0);
}
```

You can save this code in your system and use it when you write any program. Now, try to compile the code and see what happens. The output will be an error. Here is a sample of the error message the compiler will throw on your screen:

```
error.c: In function `main':
error.c:6: parse error before "return"
```

The error message will tell you where the issue is in your code. The message is difficult to understand, but it does have all the information you need. Let us break the output down into smaller pieces to understand the error message:

- Where the error has occurred. In this instance, the error has occurred before the word return.

- The error occurs in line 5 of the code

- The code with the error is saved using the file name error.c

- The type of error that has occurred

You may not have identified the issue in the code, but the compiler does give you enough evidence to help you identify the error in the code. The error is in the fifth line of the code, but unfortunately, the compiler does not identify it until it moves to the sixth line. It is also important to understand the type of error made. If there is a parse or syntax error, this means that some language punctuation is missing, and two lines of code that cannot run together are running together. The issue here is that a semicolon is not present at the end of the fifth line.

Edit the source code file and fix the issue. When you look at line number 6, you will see nothing wrong with the code and would probably wonder where the error was. Once you get the hang of it, you can identify the errors easily and make changes whenever necessary. Make necessary changes to the code to fix issues and save this file down as the source code file on your system.

When you start working on a program, there are bound to be errors. You may not be able to identify the errors initially, but with practice, you can identify the errors and debug the program within a few minutes.

Chapter Five

Analysis of Algorithms

It is important to assess the complexity of the algorithm. When it comes to analyzing an algorithm, use the asymptotic aspect to assess the algorithm. This means that you will look at how the functions in the algorithm work with large volumes of data. Donald Knuth coined the phrase "analysis of algorithms."

Computational complexity theory is based on the analysis of algorithms. You obtain a theoretical estimation of the resources required to perform an algorithm. From the previous chapters, you may have learned the input defined in any algorithm must be of an arbitrary length. If you analyze any algorithm, you must look at the time and space in the memory you need for its execution.

The running time or efficiency of an algorithm is stated as a variable of the time complexity function, and the memory used is stated as a variable of the space complexity function.

Importance of Analysis

You may be wondering why you must analyze an algorithm. We will do this using an example of a problem that can be solved in multiple ways. When you consider an algorithm to solve a specific problem, you can develop a pattern that will allow you to recognize similar problems that you can solve using this algorithm.

It is important to understand the difference between these algorithms since the objective of each is the same. The time and memory used by each algorithm will be different. For example, if you want to sort a list of numbers, you know you can use a sort algorithm. You can choose from different sort and search algorithms, and the time taken for comparison will be different for each algorithm. This means the time complexity of the algorithm can differ. You must also consider the space the algorithm will occupy in the memory.

It is important to analyze the algorithm to understand how effectively it can solve problems. You must consider the size of the memory the algorithm uses to solve a problem. However, the main concern of any algorithm is the performance and time required to run the algorithm. Perform the tests and analyses listed below to assess the performance of an algorithm:

- **Worst-case**: You should use the maximum number of steps to obtain the expected output for a given input

- **Amortized**: You can apply a sequence of operations to the input over a period of time

- **Average case**: You should use an average of the minimum and maximum number of steps to obtain the desired output for a given input

- **Best-case**: You should use a minimum number of steps to obtain the expected output for a given input

To solve any problem, you must consider the space and time complexity. The program will be executed in a system with limited memory, but there is enough space to store the data. Bear in mind that the opposite will also hold true regarding algorithms. When you compare a bubble sort and merge sort algorithm, you will see the former will need more space to store a variable. Having said that, a bubble sort algorithm will take more time than the merge sort algorithm. This means you can use the merge sort algorithm to perform a sorting function in an environment where you do not have enough time and the bubble sort algorithm if you do not have enough memory.

Analysis Methods

To assess how an algorithm is used to measure the consumption of resources, use the strategies listed below.

Asymptotic Analysis

This type of analysis assesses how the algorithm will behave if the input size constantly changes. We ignore any small value of the input variable and only focus on the larger value when we perform this analysis. The algorithm is usually better if the asymptotic growth rate is very slow. This does not necessarily hold true in all cases. Comparison of a linear algorithm and a quadratic algorithm tells you that the linear algorithm is asymptotically better since it does not use too many variables to meet the objective.

Using Recurrence Equations

Different recurrence equations can be used to describe how an algorithm will function with smaller input values. This form of analysis is performed to analyze and test divide and conquer algorithms.

Let us assume the following:

- Function T(n): used to define the running time on any problem

- N: Input size of the problem

If the value of n is small and consistent across all subproblems, the solution will take a constant time that is written as $\theta(1)$.

Let us also assume you have numerous subproblems in your algorithm, and the input size of those problems is n/b. If we want to solve the problem, the algorithm will take the time T(n/b) * a.

To calculate the time taken, use the following equation:

$$T(n) = \{\theta(1)\,aT(nb) + D(n) + C(n)\,if\,n \leqslant c\,otherwise\,T(n) = \{\theta(1)\,if\,n \leqslant ca\,T(nb) + D(n) + C(n)$$

You can also solve a recurrence relation using the following methods:

- **Recursion Tree Method**: Using a decision tree, you can view the cost of each method used

- **Substitution Method**: When you use this method, assume a bound or range and use mathematical induction to determine if your assumption is accurate

- **Master's Theorem**: This technique will enable you to identify the complexity of any recurrence relation

Amortized Analysis

This type of analysis is often performed on those algorithms with similar option sequences. You can obtain a bound or range of the cost of running the entire algorithm through amortized analysis. You do not specify a range or bound on the operations performed separately. This is a very different type of analysis, but this method is often used to analyze the efficiency of an algorithm and design the algorithm itself.

Aggregate Method

In this method, you consider the problem and look at it holistically. Let us assume that you have n operations that run when you execute an algorithm, and the time taken by these n operations is T(n). The amortized cost is T(n)/n for each operation in the algorithm, and the variable represents the worst-case scenario.

Accounting Method

In the accounting method, you must only assign a certain cost or charge to any operation performed depending on the actual cost of doing those operations. If the actual cost of the operation is lower than the amortized cost, the difference is the credit. You can then use this credit later to pay for other operations whose actual cost is greater than the amortized cost. You can calculate the cost using the following formula:

$$\sum_{i=1}^{n} c1^{\wedge} \geqslant \sum_{i=1}^{n} ci \sum_{i=1}^{n} c1^{\wedge} \geqslant \sum_{i=1}^{n} ci$$

Potential Method

This method represents the work the algorithm has completed in the form of potential energy. This method is like the accounting method, but here we look at the total cost of the algorithm in the form of its energy.

Let us assume the following:

- D_0: indicates the data structure used in the algorithm

- N: indicates the number of operations performed in an algorithm

If the cost of the operation is x and the data structure for the ith operation is represented as D_i, the amortized cost for the ith operation can be represented as:

$$c1^{\wedge} = ci + \Phi(Di) - \Phi(Di-1) \quad c1^{\wedge} = ci + \Phi(Di) - \Phi(Di-1)$$

Therefore, the total amortized cost is:

$$\sum_{i=1}^{n} c1^{\wedge} = \sum_{i=1}^{n} (ci + \Phi(Di) - \Phi(Di-1)) = \sum_{i=1}^{n} ci + \Phi(Dn) - \Phi(D0) \sum_{i=1}^{n} c1^{\wedge} = \sum_{i=1}^{n} (ci + \Phi(Di) - \Phi(Di-1)) = \sum_{i=1}^{n} ci + \Phi(Dn) - \Phi(D0)$$

40

Dynamic Table

If you run an algorithm on a system, it may not have enough memory to store the input and output variables. In such cases, you may need to remove some data from the algorithm and move it into a large table. You can also remove the information from this table or replace data whenever necessary. You can reallocate the data to move to a smaller table. You can calculate the cost of constant insertion and deletion of records from a table and determine if it exceeds a certain threshold you have in mind through amortized analysis.

Space Complexities

As mentioned earlier, every algorithm will occupy some space in the memory, especially during the execution. This section will look at how you can deal with the complex calculations that will help you assess the space that any algorithm requires. Space complexity is like time complexity and allows you to solve different classification problems of algorithms based on the computational difficulties.

It is important to look at the space complexity function when you analyze an algorithm. This function determines the space being used by the algorithm when it runs. This space may be occupied by the input, temporary, or output variable used in the algorithm. When you design algorithms, you should think about the extra memory you need to store the output and the input. Most programmers forget about the latter.

Use fixed-length variables to measure these input variables. You can either use a definite number of integers or bytes to describe the memory. Any function you define to do this is going to be independent of the actual memory space. People often ignore the space complexity, but they forget that this is as important as the time complexity since the program will not function well if there is no space in your memory.

Understanding Recursion

We looked at a simple recursive algorithm earlier in the book, but what do you know about recursion? This section will look at a recursive algorithm and give you some information to help you easily identify such algorithms.

Any recursive function is a black box. You only know what the function does but not exactly what happens. This means you only see what is expected of you to see. For instance, if you want to use a function where you sort the elements in an array, you can describe it in the following manner: 'Use the merge sort algorithm to sort the elements in one array in the ascending order using another array.'

It is also good to break this algorithm down into smaller problems and solve them before you look at the bigger problem. For example, you can say the machine has to sort the elements in one array independently and then move them into another array. Or you can break the array down and sort the elements in the array before you combine all of them into one array.

You can use the same description and apply it to any sorting algorithm, including merge sort and quick sort. The only difference between these algorithms is the way the data is divided and sorted. Quick sort uses complex partitioning methods and simple merging techniques, while merge sort is the opposite.

It is also important to describe boundary conditions when you use a recursive algorithm to stop recursion. Continuing with the example above, when you break the array into sequences, you may have some smaller arrays with only one or two elements in them. You do not have to sort such an array. When you use the insertion sort algorithm, you use the divide and conquer algorithm to break the sequence into smaller sequences and then sort the elements in those sequences before you combine the entire list.

You must remember to explain the algorithm when you talk about its overview. This is the only way to determine the functions and methods to use. Regardless of which algorithmic strategy you want to use, you must provide some description. Also, explain why you chose to use this method over the other methods.

Chapter Six

An Introduction
to Writing Programs

As someone new to programming, you need to keep some points in mind before converting an algorithm into a program. This chapter introduces you to these concepts and explains to you how one can work with different operators and data types to perform functions.

Principles of Programming

Programmers often write code for specific projects or tasks. So, they tend to write code they or someone who knows how to code will understand. There may be times when the programmer does not understand what he has written because of a change in his writing style. So, when you revisit the code, wouldn't it be easier to read something easy to understand?

The following are some principles to consider when it comes to writing programs. It is best to keep these points in mind to ensure you write high-quality code.

Naming Conventions

It is very important to stick to this principle when you write code. You must name functions, methods, and variables correctly to ensure there are no errors in the code.

Let us assume that a new programmer is checking your code. The person should find the variables and understand their function by looking at your code. Name the variables based on the domain and functionality of the method or project. It is also important to use the word 'is' as a prefix to a Boolean variable.

For example, if you are working on an application for a bank to deal with payments, you can use the following variables:

```
double totalBalance;        // Represents
the user account balance
double amountToDebit;       // Represents the
amount to charge the user
double amountToCredit;   // Represents the
amount to give to the user
boolean isUserActive;
```

Stick to the following naming conventions:

- You must use the camel case to label data structures and variables. For example,

```
int  integerArray[] = new int[10];
String  merchantName = "Perry Mason";
```

- Using the screaming snake case to label constants. For example,

```
final long int ACCOUNT_NUMBER = 123456;
```

File Structure

The coder must maintain the structure of the project. It will be easy to understand the code when you stick to the structure. The structure is very different for different kinds of applications. The idea will, however, remain the same. For example,

Looking at Functions and Methods

If you use the right methods and functions in your code, you will be an expert at programming. Stick to the following rules when you name functions:

- Use camel case to name a function or method

- The method name should be on the same line as the opening bracket of the method

- Name functions using a non-verb sound

- Ensure that the functions only use one or two arguments at the most

For example,

```
double getUserBalance(long int
accountNumber) {
// Method Definition
}
```

Indentation

If you want to use abstract classes or write some lines outside of a method, it indicates you want to nest the code. If you have not written the code, it becomes tricky to understand what goes where. It is difficult to work with such code because you never know where something ends unless you use indentation. Therefore, you should stick to the indentation. All this means is that you use the brackets in the right place.

Avoid Self-Explanation

As a programmer, you are expected to write comments against your code. You must explain what a method or function is expected to do. Do not write self-explanatory comments because that is useless and does not add any value to the code. It is important to write code that everybody understands. For example,

```
final double PI = 3.14; // This is pi value
//
```

Do you think the above statement needs a comment? It does not because it says the variable holds the value of Pi, and this is self-explanatory.

KISS

KISS is an acronym for Keep It Simple Silly. The US Navy coined this principle in 1960. This principle states that any system that you develop should always be kept as simple as possible. Avoid adding unnecessary complexities to the code. The question you must ask yourself while writing code is – "Can this code be written in a better and easier way?" This is the only way the code will be readable and easy for anybody to understand.

DRY

DRY is an acronym for Don't Repeat Yourself, and this is like the previous principle. Ensure the code you write is unambiguous. The compiler should not spend too much time trying to decipher. This is the only way you can avoid repeating your lines of code to help the compiler understand what you want it to do.

YAGNI

According to the YAGNI (You Aren't Gonna Need It) principle, any functions and operations should be added to the code only if it is necessary. This is a part of the extreme programming methodology where you can choose to improve the code you write by sticking to only what is most necessary. Use this principle in conjunction with unit testing, integration, and refactoring.

Logging

When you write code, it does not mean the code will be written well or that it will compile successfully. You will need to debug the code and test it to ensure it runs smoothly. If you have large programs, it will take longer to debug. So, you need to break the code and then test it. When you test a piece of code, create a log. When you write a log statement, you can use those statements to help you debug the code. It is a good idea to write a log statement in a function. Since most of the processing is done only through a function or method, it is best to write the log statement to understand whether the function is a success or failure.

Objects and Classes

Classes

A class is a blueprint, and you can create an object from the class. A class has one of these variable types:

- Class – These are declared in a class and outside a method using the static keyword.

- Class variables – Class variables are declared in classes, not inside any method, using the static keyword.

- Local variables– These variables are defined inside a block, method, or constructor and hence are called local variables. You should declare this variable in the class and initialize it in the method. Once the method runs fully, it will be removed from the computer memory

- Instance – This is a variable that has been defined inside a class but outside a method. They are initialized at the time of class instantiation, and they can be accessed from within a method, block, or constructor of the class.

Classes can have multiple methods for accessing the values of different methods. In the case of a person, eating() is a method.

Objects

Objects are present around you. These include dogs, humans, buildings, houses, etc. Every object has its own characteristics, behavior, and state. For instance, consider a dog. Some of its characteristics and states include name, color, breed, etc., while its behaviors include running, barking, and tail wagging. Look at a software object in a similar manner. You will see there is not too much of a difference between the two. Every software object also has its own state and behavior. The state is stored in a field, and a method indicates the behavior.

Creating Objects

As mentioned earlier, an object comes from the class, and you can use the new keyword to describe the object in the class. Follow the steps below to create an object:

- **Declaration**: Declare a variable with a name and define the object type in the code

- **Instantiation:** We use the new keyword to create an object

- **Initialization**: A call to a constructor follows the new keyword, and this will initialize the object

If you want to access an instance method or variable, you must create an object. Use the following path for the instance variable:

```
/* First create the object */
ObjectReference = new Constructor();
/* Now call the variable like this */
ObjectReference.variableName;
/* Now you may call the class method like
this */
ObjectReference.MethodName();
```

Constructors

A constructor is a very important part of a class. Every class has one, and if we don't write one for our class, Java will provide a default constructor. When you create a new object in a class, the compiler automatically invokes the constructor. The primary rule for a constructor is that it must have an identical name to the class, and a class may have more than one constructor.

Every programming language allows you to use a singleton class, and you can use these to create only one instance of a class.

How to Declare Source Files

It is important to understand the rules of source files, especially when you declare a class in the code. An import statement and a package statement in a source file are important to assess.

- A source file may have as many non-public classes as you want

- In a class that has been defined in a package, the first statement in the source file must be the package statement

- You may only have one public class in any source file

- If included, import statements should be written between the class declaration and the package statement. If there is no package statement, the import statement will be the first line of the source file

- The source file and the public class must have the same name, with the file name appended with the extension of the programming language

- Package and import statements imply to every class that is present in the source file. You cannot declare different ones or different classes

A package is a categorization of the class and interface – this must be done when you are programming, just to make life easier for yourself.

The import statement provides the right location for the compiler to find a specific class.

Data Types

Data is a representation of various instructions, concepts, and facts. This information is in a specific format and can be used for interpretation, communication, or processing by the machine. Special characters and groups of other characters are used to represent this data.

Any classified or organized data is known as information. Information is processed data, and every decision or action is based on this information. This information will have some meaning to it, which is what the receiver is looking for. If the decision being made should be meaningful, the processed data should meet the following criteria:

- Completeness: The information should have all the parameters and data

- Accuracy: The information should always be accurate

- Timely: The information should always be available whenever required

Data Processing Cycle

The data processing involves the re-ordering or the restructuring of the data by the machine. This will help increase the use of the data and add value to the purpose. There are three steps that constitute the data processing cycle:

Input

In this step, the data is fed into the machine, and you need to prepare the input data and change it to a form the machine can read easily. The structure that you will need to use depends on the type of machine being used. For instance, when you use electronic computers, you can record the input data using different types of media like magnetic disks, pen drives, tapes, and more.

Processing

In this step, the data from the previous step is re-structured to produce information or data that can be more useful. For instance, a paycheck is calculated based on the time cards or the number of hours that people spend at work. Similarly, the summary of sales can be calculated based on the sales orders.

Output

This is the final step of the processing cycle, and the data from the previous step is collected in this step. You can decide what the format of the data should be depending on the use of the data.

A variable is a reserved location in memory used for storing values. When you create a new variable, you automatically reserve that space in the memory. The amount of memory is determined by the type of the variable – the operating system allocates the memory and determines what may be stored in it. You can store decimals, integers, or characters by assigning a different type to a variable. Every programming language has two main data types:

- Primitive

- Reference or object

Primitive

Most high-level programming languages contain eight primitive data types. These are predefined by the language and are named with a keyword. The eight types are:

int

The int has a default of zero, a maximum value of 2,147,483,647, while the minimum is -2147,483,647. It is normally used as the default type for integral values unless memory is short.

long

The long has a default of 0L, with a maximum value of 9, 223,372,036,854,775,808 and minimum of - 9,223,372,036,854,775,807. It is used when you need a longer range than the int provides.

float

The float has a default of 0.0f and is generally used to save some memory when you have large arrays containing floating-point numbers. It is never used when you need a precise value, such as for currency.

double

The double has a default value of 0.0d. It is used normally as the decimal value type and should never be used for any values that are precise, like currency.

byte

A byte is a data type with a default value of 0. The minimum value is -128, while the maximum is 127. It is used for saving space in the larger arrays, usually instead of an integer, because an integer is four times larger than the byte.

short

A short is a data type with a default value of 0. The minimum value is -32,768, while the maximum is 32,767. It may also be used for saving memory as a byte data type. The integer is two times bigger than the short.

boolean

The boolean is used to represent a single piece of information and has just two values – true or false. It is used when you need to track either true or false conditions. Its default value is false.

char

The char data type may be used for the storage of any character

Reference Data Types

We use constructors to create reference variables. The reference variable is used to access an object and is declared as specific types known as immutable. This means they cannot be changed once declared. Reference objects include class objects and a variety of array variables. The default value of any reference variable is null, and it can be used to refer to other objects.

Literals

Literals are a source code representation of fixed values represented in the code directly without the need for any computation. You can assign a literal as the primitive data type in the following way:

```
byte a = 67;
char a = 'A'
```

You can also express int, byte, short, and long in octal, decimal, or hexadecimal number systems. We must include 'o' before the number to indicate the octal system and '0x' to indicate the hexadecimal system. For example:

```
int decimal = 100;
```

```
int octal = 0144;
int hexa =  0x64;
```

String literals are specified in the code, similar to how they are specified in other languages. It is a sequence of characters enclosed in a set of double quotes. Some programming languages allow you to use char and string literals with escape sequences. The following are some to use:

Escape Sequence	Representation
\n	Newline
\r	Carriage return
\f	Form Feed
\b	Backspace
\s	Space
\t	tab
\"	Double quote
\'	Single quote
\\	backslash
\ddd	Octal character
\uxxxx	

Operations

Different operators can be used to manipulate data and variables in any code. In this section, we will look at different operators and their functions.

Logical

Operator	Description
&& (logical and)	evaluates true if both operands are non-zero values
|| (logical or)	evaluates true if either operand is non-zero
! (logical not)	evaluates false if a condition is true because it reverses the logical state of the operand

Arithmetic

These are used for mathematical expressions in much the same way you used the same symbols at school:

Operator	Description
+	Addition for adding values on the left or right of the operator

-	Subtraction for subtracting the right operand from the left
*	Multiplication for multiplying values on the left or right of the operator
/	Division for dividing the left operand by the right operand
%	Modulus, the remainder of the division of the left operand by the right operand
++	Increment, for increasing an operand value by 1
--	Decrement, for decreasing an operand value by 1

Assignment

Operator	Description
=	assigns the value from the right operand to the left
+=	adds the value of the right operand to the left and assigns the result to the left
-=	subtracts the right from the left operand

	and assigns the result to the left
*=	multiplies the right with the left operand and assigns the result to the left
/=	divides the left operand with the right and assigns the result to the left
%=	takes the modulus of two operands and assigns the result to the left
<<=	left shift and assignment
>>=	right shift and assignment

Relational

There are several relational operators in a programming language:

Operator	Description
== (equal to)	checks if the values of the operands are equal; evaluates true if they are
!= (not equal to)	checks if the values of the operands are equal; evaluates true if not
> (greater than)	checks if the left operand is greater

	than the right; evaluates true if it is
< (less than)	checks if the left operand is less than the right; evaluates true if it is
>= (greater than or equal to)	checks if the left operand is greater than or the same as the right; evaluates true if it is
<= (less than or equal to)	checks if the left operand is less than or the same as the right; evaluates true if it is

Operator Precedence

Every programming language has operator precedence to determine how expressions are evaluated by looking at their variables. Some operators have higher precedence than others, such as multiplication over addition. For instance:

```
x = 6 + 2 * 3
```

Here, if you calculate the value of x, you may say 24. Since multiplication is higher in the precedence order, the processor or compiler will calculate this as 2*3 and then add the 6. Here, the operators are in order of their precedence from highest to lowest.

In any expression those operators with the highest precedence will be the first ones evaluated:

Category	Operator	Associativity
Postfix	>() [] . (dot operator)	Left to right
Unary	>++ - - ! ~	Right to left
Multiplicative	>* /	Left to right
Additive	>+ -	Left to right
Shift	>>> >>> <<	Left to right
Relational	>> >= < <=	Left to right
Equality	>== !=	Left to right
Logical AND	>&&	Left to right
Logical OR	>||	Left to right
Conditional	?:	Right to left
Assignment	>= += -= *= /= %= >>= <<= &= ^= |=	Right to left

Chapter Seven

Types of Programming Languages

Many programming languages exist, and many are being developed to serve different purposes. Some examples include R and Python. These languages are being developed for the purpose of data analytics. Since different programming languages are now available for use, it is important to understand the pros and cons of the language and its characteristics. You can classify programming languages into different types based on the style of programming you want to use. Multiple programming languages are implemented every year, but only some of these are popular now. Professional programmers are using them in their careers.

You can use programming languages to control the performance of the machine and computer. As mentioned earlier, each programming language is different, and we will look at the different types of programming languages in this chapter. Based on the information in this chapter, you can determine the type of programming language you can use.

Definition

Before we look at different types of programming languages, let us understand what a programming language is. A programming language is one used to instruct a machine or computer to perform specific functions. Some programmers call these languages notations. These languages are used to express algorithms and control the performance of a machine.

It is for this reason you can write an algorithm using different programming languages. There are close to a thousand programming languages developed, and some are used more often than others. These languages could either have an imperative or declarative form, depending on how you would use the language. You can also divide the program into two forms – syntax and semantics.

Types of Programming Languages

In this section, we will look at different types of programming languages. Every programming language will fall under one of these categories.

Procedural Programming Language

This type of programming language is often used by programmers who use an algorithm and define the sequence of instructions or statements that they use to instruct the machine. This type of language uses heavy loops, multiple variables, and a few other elements. For this reason, this language is different from the next type of programming language - functional programming language.

A procedural programming language can be used to control variables dependent on the values returned by a method or function. For instance, syntaxes and statements in this type of language can be used to print information.

Functional Programming Language

A functional programming language is dependent on any stored data or information in the computer, and it uses recursive functions instead of loops. The objective of this type of programming language is to only use the return values of any method or function.

Logic Programming Language

This type of programming language allows any programmer or developer to use declarative statements. A logic programming language gives the machine a chance to understand and compile the instructions to perform necessary functions. If you use this type of programming language, you do not have to instruct the computer on how to perform a certain function. The language uses efficient algorithms, making it easy for the computer to use less space. All you must do is employ some restrictions on how the machine should think.

Programming Languages

Pascal Language

Pascal is a programming language most students learn during school, and not many industries still use this programming language. The Pascal language, unlike most languages, does not use braces and symbols but uses key phrases and words. This is why it is easy for beginners to learn this language compared to other languages, such as C and C++. Pascal also supports object-oriented programming through Delphi. Borland, a software company, only uses this language.

Fortran Language

Fortran is a language most scientists use since it is easier to use to crunch numbers. This language allows you to store variables easily regardless of the memory size of the variable. Data scientists or engineers use this language to calculate values or make predictions with high accuracy. It is difficult to write programs in this language, and the core written is sometimes hard to understand. So, you would need to learn and understand the language if you want to code using it.

Java Language

Java is a multi-platform language and is used to perform different networking functions. This application is used on Java-based web applications. Since this language has a format and syntax that is like C++, developers can use this language to develop applications on cross platforms. If you have mastered C++ programming, Java will come naturally to you. Java is also an object-oriented programming language, and therefore, can be used to develop different products and applications. The older versions of Java do not allow you to write heavy code, but the latest versions have some features that make it easier to write effective and shorter programs.

Perl Language

Perl is a language often used in the Unix operating system. It is often used to manage files and directories. This language is more popular for its Common Gateway Interface or CGI programming feature. CGI is used to define the programs used by web servers to provide additional capabilities to different websites and pages. It is also used to look for text and monitor databases and server functions. It is a simple language, and you can easily pick up the language's fundamentals. Since the language is CGI, most web hosting services prefer to use the Perl language instead of C++ since a Perl script file can host numerous websites.

PHP Language

This language, primarily a scripting language, is used to design web applications and pages. Since this language is used to develop web pages or applications, it comprises features to link the websites to different databases, recreate or restructure a website or generate HTTP headers. PHP also includes a set of components since it is a scripting language, and the components permit the developer to use some object-oriented features. These features make it easier to develop websites.

LISP Language

Many programmers use this language since this language allows you to store different types of data structures, such as lists and arrays. The syntax of the data structures being used is easy to understand and simple. This is why it can be used to create new data structures and perform functions you cannot perform using other programming languages.

Scheme Language

The Scheme programming language is an alternative or substitute to LISP, and it has simple features. The syntax used in the language is easy to learn. If you want to develop programs or products using this language, you can also re-implement it in other languages, especially LISP. This is a basic programming language and is often used only to solve simple problems, especially those where you do not have to worry about the syntax of the language.

C++ Language

The C++ language is an object-oriented programming language, and it is for this reason that programmers use this language when they have to build large applications. A programmer can break a complex program into smaller sections making it easier for them to work on smaller programs. Since this is an object-oriented programming language, you can use one block of code multiple times. Some say that this language is efficient, but there are others who will not agree.

C Language

C is a very common programming language, and almost anybody can easily learn and code in this language. Most programmers prefer to use this language since programs run faster. The language uses different features, and these features allow programmers to develop efficient programs using the right algorithms. This language is used only because it allows people to use some features from C++.

In this chapter, we looked at different programming languages, such as Pascal, Fortran, C, C++, Scheme, and others, and learned how they can be used. We also looked at the differences between these languages. Many languages have also been developed that are similar to the languages listed above. You need to know which language works best for the program or product you are developing.

Chapter Eight

Important Programming Techniques

Since numerous programming languages are being developed, it becomes difficult to determine which language is the best to use. Every programming language can be used for different reasons. This, however, should not matter since the syntax used in any language is more important. It is also important to determine how you work on solving the problem. It is always about algorithmic thinking. Learn to break the problem into different steps and see how you can solve these problems.

While it is important to understand the syntax, it is very important to understand how any programming language is structured. You must know what different terms mean and how they can be used.

Arrays

Arrays are collections of variables with the same data type. Every element is assigned an index, and it is best to use these indices to look up the elements in the array. For example, you can create random numbers, so if you want any random item like the day of the week, you can use the index to pull out the random number.

Some programming languages do not support the use of data structures like arrays. You can, however, replicate the functionalities of an array using lists or tuples. You can use binary trees in an array if the array is sparsely populated. It is messy to do this, but it is easier to do this if you want to use different types of data. JavaScript allows you to use the array index as a Boolean operator, and this means you can use various binary expressions to evaluate the condition. This makes it easier to select the values without using any conditional statements.

An array is also known as a multivariable since it allows you to store different variables of the same data type together. You can declare arrays in your program the same way you declare other variables in the program:

```
float array1[10];
```

In the example above, we assign an array with the length 10, indicating it can hold 10 values. You can define or add values to the array using the following line:

```
Float array1[] = {53.0, 88.0, 96.7, 93.1,
89.5};
```

This array contains five values that are of the float data type.

- You can refer to every element in the array as an independent variable when you use it in a function or module. The items in the array are known as elements

- Every element is given a specific position, and this position is known as the index. The index of the first element in the array is zero, and in the example above, the first number 53.0 is at position zero

- You can assign the values to the array the same way you assign values to regular variables

- Every program has a fixed array size, and when you determine the dimension of an array, by assigning the array a length

Building Big Programs

You can write small or big programs. While there is no harm with writing big programs, you should understand the computer would take some time to compile the code. It will take longer to identify the errors and edit the code. This would mean the program is going to have errors, and you should accept it.

If you want to write big programs, see if you can break it down into smaller segments. You can use pointers to connect the smaller segments and create a program flow. For example, a module may declare variables, while another may initialize them, while another could be used to perform some functions on the variables and display the results. This is why it becomes easier to debug the program and identify errors if required. Another advantage of doing this is that you can use these smaller modules in the future, which will help you save time.

If the compiler runs the source code file, it may create an object code that will be linked to various libraries in the programming language. It will then produce a file it can easily execute. This is how the linking works between the compiler and the linker. Variables can be shared across different modules or source codes, and a number of functions can be performed on those variables.

Bitwise Logic

If you use bitwise logic to write code, you can either set or unset bits. Some programming languages also allow you to mask some bits in your code. This is a programming staple that everyone must know. You can combine numerous values into binary flags and save these flags in the machine's memory. This means code does not require large chunks of memory to save data. This is a great method to combine values that you can pass between methods and functions as only one argument.

Bitwise logic can also be used to pass different values between web pages and other programs using cookies or query strings. You can also use this method as a simple and quick way to convert the variables from the denary to the binary system. Bitwise logic can be used to encipher text, as well.

Boolean Logic

If you wish to combine different values, it is important for one to learn about AND, OR, NOT, etc. These operators will make it easier to create and develop truth tables. A Boolean operator is often used all of the time by programmers. One of the most important things to consider is that every expression must be evaluated as true or false. You need to determine the syntax to use based on the language that you choose to write in.

Closures

Closures are anonymous functions that can also be used as code blocks. These blocks can be passed outside any method or function. This code will capture all the variables from the function or inner block. This might sound a little complicated, but it is definitely easy to understand using an example. In the example below, we will see how to use closures in programming:

```
func makeIncrementer(forIncrement amount:
Int) -> () -> Int {
    var runningTotal = 0
    func incrementer() -> Int {
        runningTotal += amount
        return runningTotal
    }
    return incrementer
}
let incrementByTen =
makeIncrementer(forIncrement: 10)
print("\(incrementByTen())")
print("\(incrementByTen())")
print("\(incrementByTen())")
```

The output of the above code is 10, 20, and 30. The output changes since the function makeIncrementer() uses the value 10 as the base. This value is then added to the total using the function incrementbyTen(). You can also create another incrementer function if you want to increase the value by 5.

74

```
let incrementByFive =
makeIncrementer(forIncrement: 5)
```

If you run this function thrice, the compiler will throw 5, 10, and 15 as the output. The makeIncrementer() function works behind the scenes and creates the instance of a class by passing the values to add. The benefit of using closures is to build code that is easier to understand. Reduce the cognitive load making the code easier to compile and implement.

Concurrency

The concept of concurrency is very different from parallel computing. The concepts are similar, but the difference is in parallel computing, the code runs on different processes at the same time. If you use concurrency, the program can be split into different segments, and each segment is executed separately. You can do this even if the program is running and functioning correctly.

Many programming languages use the concept of multithreading, but it is better to use the concept of concurrency to write code. Concurrency ensures fewer errors in the code. For example, if you were to code in C#, use the Task Parallel Library or TPL to add some elements of concurrency to the code. This method uses the CLR thread pool to run multiple processes allowing you to run the program without having to create threads, which is a very costly operation. You can chain various tasks together and run them together to obtain the results.

It is best to use asynchronous code if you want since it allows you to run programs at the same time without hampering the functioning of other code. When you use asynchronous code to make some web service calls, the code runs without blocking the thread. The thread can continue to respond to any other requests while it waits for the first few requests to complete. In the example below, we will see how to use asynchronous code and concurrency to perform functions.

```
public async Task MethodAsync()
{
    Task longRunningTask =
LongRunningTaskAsync();
    ... any code here

    int result = await longRunningTask;
    DoSomething(result);
}

public async Task LongRunningTaskAsync() {
// returns an int
    await Task.Delay(1000);
    return 1;
}
```

At times, a programmer may choose to use different pages to access information at the same time. While the compiler fetches a page, it will process it. It is impossible to determine how the pages are processed, and the order in which the compiler performs this function since every language uses the process of concurrency to perform this activity.

Decision or Selection

Never write a program that only performs one action. It is important to ensure the code you write is flexible and can be updated to suit other needs if needed. So, you must write code that will accept user inputs and perform the functions based on that input. Use different statements, such as selection or if-else statements, to use any input and perform a function or action based on the condition. You can use lists and arrays, as well.

Disk Access

Most people use computers to store data and information and work on that information in the future. Every programming language has a number of functions that can be used to read and write information to and from the disk. Any program you write is saved on your computer's disk, but this will only happen if you have used the file save command to write the code.

Immutability

If you declare some variables as immutable in your code, you cannot change them. Some programming languages allow you to determine the immutability of a variable using specific prefixes. You should, however, ensure you do not have any dependencies to the variable. You can always change the declaration if you need to. In the example below, we will look at how to declare variables with immutable properties. We will also declare some fields as immutable.

```
class Person {
```

```
let firstName: String
let lastName: String

init(first: String, last: String) {
    firstName = first
    lastName = last
}

public func toString() -> String {
    return "\(self.firstName)
\(self.lastName)";
}
}

var man = Person(first:"David",
last:"Bolton")
print( man.toString() )
The output of the code is "David Bolton."
```

If you want to change the first or last name in the code, the compiler will throw an error. It is important to use immutable variables in the code. Using these variables, the compiler optimizes the output. The immutable data type will never change if you use a multi-threaded programming language. The value of the variable is shared between different modules and threads. If you want to copy the value of an immutable object, you must only copy the reference to that variable and not the variable itself.

Interacting with the Command Line

The main function or method in the code works very differently in the code. It is what the compiler relies on when going through the entire code. Every function in the code will communicate with the command line, and this is the only way the code you write communicates with the computer. Another way the program can communicate is by reading the instructions from the command line.

Interacting with the OS

Every programming allows you to work with the operating system to perform some functions. Through these languages, you can create new directories, change directories, rename files, create files, delete files, and perform other handy tasks on the operating system.

You can also run other programs using one single program. The easiest way to do this is to use pointers. You can locate the right program in the memory using pointers. You can also use the program to examine the results of a function performed by the operating system. It is an easy-to-use program that interacts with other programs and examines the efficiency of your computer. If you know how to add code, you can easily perform all these functions.

Lambdas

This expression is the best way to call on an anonymous function in the code while the program is running. A lambda is a useful method to use with languages that will allow you to support different kinds of first-class functions. It is easy to pass the function or any other module as a parameter in a different function. This indicates you can easily pass functions and return them as functions if needed. A lambda originated with different functional languages like C# and Lisp. The following syntax is used to create a lambda function:

()-> {code...}

Many languages, including PHP, Swift, Java, JavaScript, Python, and VB.NET, support lambda functions. It is important to understand how lambda functions can be used. A lambda function can make the code shorter and extremely easy to understand. Consider the following example where we are trying to build a list of the odd numbers:

```
    List list = new List() { 1, 2, 3, 4, 5,
6, 7, 8 };
    List oddNumbers = list.FindAll(x => (x %
2) != 0);
The oddNumbers will contain the numbers 1,
3, 5 and 7
```

Loops and Repetitions

This is another important technique that you should consider when writing code. The for loop is the most common type of loop or repetition that people write in their programs. Some coders also choose to use the while loop when they code. The while loop does complicate the solution. In most programming languages, the for loop will use the idea of counting the number of iterations. How the iterations occur and the variables that are considered are dependent on the programming language.

Linked Lists

Most programmers worry about using linked lists since they are slightly difficult to understand. A linked list is a strange concept since the user must know how a pointer can be used in a linked list and how this pointer works. Linked lists combine the functions of an array with pointers and structures. One can say that a linked list is like an array of structures. Unlike a data structure, such as an array or list, the user can easily remove the linked list elements.

Modular Arithmetic

In modular arithmetic, you divide the number and use different operations to obtain results. This is the best way to limit the output you obtain from a method or function. Different modular arithmetic functions can also be used to wrap things around, and it is for this reason this technique is useful. You must understand this technique well, especially if you want to use it the right way in your code.

Pointers

Most programming languages use pointers, which are used to manipulate different variables stored in a computer's memory. You may be wondering why you would want to use a pointer to navigate to a certain part in your memory, but using a pointer allows you to change the value of any variable using an operator or function. Pointers give programming languages more power when compared to other programming languages. It does take some time to understand how to use pointers and what you can do to variables using pointers. You can declare pointers using an asterisk. You must ensure the compiler does not confuse this asterisk with the multiplication operation. Assign a pointer before you use it.

Safe Calls

Sir Tony Hoare, a computer scientist, once said you should never introduce a null reference to your code since this will only lead to errors in the output. If you access a variable using a null reference, it will lead to an exception unless you have the right handler in place. The program or system will otherwise crash. It is best to use programming languages with exception handlers to avoid recurring errors in your code. Some high-level programming languages, like C, cannot identify null pointers in the code, and this can lead to errors in the output.

Numerous programming languages include safety checks that will prevent any null reference errors. For example, in C#, you can avoid blocks of code if you have the right exception handler in place. You must use a condition to tell the compiler which lines of code to avoid. This reduces the number of lines the compiler should run in the code.

Consider the following example:

```
int? count = customers?[0]?.Orders?.Count();
```

The symbol '?' indicates to the compiler to set the value to zero if the customer variable defined in the code has a null value. Otherwise, the compiler will call upon the Count() function. If you use the function, you must declare the variable to hold a null value so you do not have an error when the code is run.

Scaling and Random Numbers

Most high-level programming languages use different types of libraries. Using these libraries, you can generate random numbers. If you use a programming language without this feature, it is best to use integers to perform different methods and functions. This will, however, not serve the purpose. Therefore, it is important to learn how to obtain random numbers and use the necessary functions to scale them. You can ensure shapes on a screen will always either increase or decrease in the same size through scaling.

Random numbers can also be used just because you want to, especially when you use different data structures. When you add a degree of randomness to these numbers, you can make the numbers look natural. For instance, if you want to draw a tree or any other object on the screen, you can use the recursion concept to do this. If you do not add some randomness to the code, the object you draw will not look like it.

Many functions in different programming languages allow you to create pseudorandom numbers. These numbers can be distributed uniformly within a range. Bear in mind this is not something you are required to do.

Strings

Strings are a common data type most programmers work with, and this is often used in any text manipulation program. We will look at what text manipulation is later in this chapter. You can define a string using an array or any other data structure but define it as a structure of characters. For instance,

```
Char name1[] = "Emma";
```

Using the above line, you can create a string variable called name1, and this variable holds the value, Emma. Since you have defined the variable as an array, the value will be saved as 'E,' 'm,' 'm', and 'a.' Alternatively, you can write the value using this format:

```
Char name1[] = { 'E', 'm', 'm', 'a'};
```

It is important to keep the following points in mind regarding strings:

- Different functions can be used to manipulate strings.

- Strings end with the null character that is defined in the library class stdio.h. `

- You can read strings using scanf() or get(). String values can be displayed using the printf() function.

- Strings are character arrays and end with the null character.

Structures

Every programming language uses a combination of different variables, and you can convert variables into different data structures. A structure is like a record in a database since it can be used to describe numerous entities at the same time. As a programmer, you can determine how to declare and initialize a data structure. Consider this example:

```
struct example
{
 int a;
char b;
float c;
}
```

In the above structure, we see three variables. Each variable is assigned a specific data type. Using this function, you can create a structure with three variables, but you do not necessarily have to declare these variables. If you would like to declare the variables, you will need to increase the number of lines in your code. A structure can also be used to work on different databases based on the type of programming language on which you are working. You should learn everything about different programming languages and structures, especially how you should usethem to write code.

Text Manipulation

Text manipulation is a key concept, and most people writing code want to learn how to manipulate characters and strings. You must understand these concepts well. If you know how to code, you know the text is stored in the number format based on the ASCII code. Therefore, you must learn how to convert any character into its ASCII code and vice versa. You can also use this number to check if the characters are upper or lower case. Using the ASCII code, you can create ciphers using bitwise EOR.

You can also break or divide strings using the left() and right() functions, and this allows you to perform different types of tasks. You can create anagrams or display the required texts on the screen. The text manipulation functions in any programming language allow you to change the case of any letter and format text so it looks a certain way when you build the code or program. You can do this to improve how your program appears.

Trigonometry

You need to understand some concepts when it comes to programming, and understanding trigonometry is one of the most important concepts of all. These topics are often used when you develop code or programs that use animation. Trigonometry is one of the most important concepts that programmers use while they develop code. The use of sine and cosine functions makes it easier to create a circular motion, draw patterns and circles, find the perfect layout for objects on a website or even identify the right angles and directions in which the objects must turn. It is difficult to compute various trigonometric functions, but they improve the efficiency of programs.

Variables

The objective of any method or function written is to obtain a result or output. If you do not use the right variables in the code, you will not get the right output. The programs you develop may be of no use to you, as well. For example, how would it feel if you developed a program to obtain the output of a mathematical function but did not receive the output because you missed a variable in the code? For this reason, you need to include variables in the code. These are the most important aspects of any programming language. The variables you use in the code, their type, the method used to declare and initialize the variable will differ between programming languages.

Chapter Nine

Testing the Program

L ike how we analyze algorithms to see if they are effective, it is important to test any code you write. Different tests and parameters can be used to perform these tests. It is important to stick to the TBB or test-driven development approach if you want to assess the code.

Laws of TTD

The following rules must be kept in mind if you choose to perform a TTD test on the code you write:

1. You should create a prototype of the code and write the test code. Run this code and compile it to see if it works well. You must do this before you write the production code

2. Ensure you do not write a very big code because the test may fail. Use smaller segments of code as test code, so it becomes easier to correct the code

3. Rewrite the test code if there are failures, compile the code and then write the production code

When you perform tests on the code, write the production code at the same time to ensure the code you write is accurate.

Keeping the Tests Clean

Ensure the tests you run are clean of any errors. If you have a test code filled with bugs, do not run that test since it is of no use to you. Bear in mind the test code should change as often as the production code changes. If the tests are dirty, it will be hard to change them. You need to design the test in the right manner. You need to be careful and think through the process. Ensure the test code is clean and a replica of the production code.

Testing the Abilities of the Code

- No matter how flexible the architecture or code is, if you do not run all the tests and ensure the code functions well, you cannot change the code. It is important to do this if you want to avoid any errors in the production code

- The unit test ensures the code is maintainable, reusable, and flexible. Only make changes to the code if you have some tests you can run to assess the changes. If you do not have any tests, debug the code every time you make a change to it

Clean Tests

Ensure any test you perform has the following attributes:

Readability

This is an important aspect to consider when you write test code. Ensure the code has all the relevant attributes and is easy for anybody to read. The code should also use simple variables and functions and define everything one must test in the code.

Testing Language

It is important to assess the functions and utilities in specialized APIs used by the test code. They make it easier to understand the test code and the purpose behind each line of code.

Dual Standard

You must consider a few things when you write the test or production code. You may not want to try these in the production code but you will try them out in the test code. This ensures the production code you write is usable.

Assertions

Any test code you write must have an assertion. This may cause some duplication in the code, but you can set the template method and leave that as the base class. You also need to use the assertions on different tests. Therefore, you must include at least one assertion when you run a test.

Characteristics of Tests

This section will look at the different aspects you must consider when you perform a test on the code.

Self-Validating

Every test should have a Boolean output to help you determine if the test works the way it should. Ensure a user does not have to go through the log to verify your written code.

Independent

None of the tests you run should have a dependence on each other. Run the tests in different orders to ensure the code works regardless of the type of environment it is in.

Timely

Ensure the tests you write can compile in a few seconds. Write the test code before you write the production code. That way, you can tweak the production code and run it without errors. If you start writing tests after you begin writing the production code, you cannot update the production code, so it does not have any errors.

Repeatable

You should try to repeat every test you perform in any environment. In case you write a test code, but it cannot perform well in other environments, you must determine why they fail.

Fast

Ensure every test you perform is fast. If the test is slow, you may not want to run it frequently because it will take up too much time. A slow test may not help you with identifying issues in your code.

Remember, the code will rot if your tests rot.

Chapter Ten

Sorting and Searching Algorithms

This chapter will look at the different sorting and searching algorithms. Since C is one of the simpler programming languages out there, we will look at implementing these algorithms in this language.

Searching Algorithms

As the name suggests, a searching algorithm finds an element in any data structure and retrieves the element and its location from that structure. There are two types of searching algorithms:

Types of Searching AlgorithmsSequential Search

A sequential search is one where the algorithm traverses through the data structure sequentially to look for the target element. It will search through each element in the data set. An example of this algorithm is the linear search algorithm.

Interval Search

An interval search algorithm searches for the element in a sorted data structure. This means you must first use a sorting algorithm on the data structure before you perform an interval search. This type of searching algorithm is effective since it searches for the target at the center of the structure. An example of this type of algorithm is the binary search algorithm, and we will look at this in further detail later in the book.

Linear Search Versus Binary Search

A linear search does not require you to sort the array, and it scans every item in the array to search for the element. It does not exclude any element in the array, either. This means the time taken by the compiler to search for an element is directly proportional to the number of elements in the data structure. For example, the algorithm will take less time to search for the element if there are only 5 elements in the array but will take longer if there are 15 elements in the array. On the other hand, a binary search reduces the time taken to search for the element in the array. We will look at these algorithms in further detail in the next section of this chapter.

Important Differences

- You should sort the array before using the binary search algorithm, but this is not required for a linear search algorithm

- Linear search follows the sequential process while the binary search algorithm will look at the data randomly

- The binary search algorithm performs comparisons based on the segment, while the linear search will perform an equality comparison

Linear Search

Using the example below, we will understand how a linear search can be performed on an array. In the problem, we will consider an array and use a function to find the element in the array. Since the linear search algorithm checks every element in the array, it will traverse through the entire data structure. It is for this reason this search algorithm is not efficient.

For instance, to look for the element 16 in an array, the algorithm will go through each element to find it.

```
Array1[] = {1, 4, 16, 5, 19, 10}
Output: 16
```

It will also return the index of the number.

Let us assume that the number is not present in the array. What do you think will happen then? Let us look for the number 45.

```
Output: -1
```

To perform a linear search algorithm, use the steps given below:

- Define the array and add numbers to it

- Identify the element you want to search for

- Begin with the leftmost element that is present in the array

- Compare the target element with each of the elements in the array

- If the target element matches the element in the array, return the index

If the target element is not present, return -1 **Implementation**

```c
#include <stdio.h>
int search(int arr[], int n, int x)
{
    int i;
    for (i = 0; i < n; i++)
        if (arr[i] == x)
            return i;
    return -1;
}

int main(void)
{
    int arr[] = { 2, 3, 4, 10, 40 };
    int x = 10;
    int n = sizeof(arr) / sizeof(arr[0]);
    int result = search(arr, n, x);
    (result == -1) ? printf("Element is not
present in array")
                    : printf("Element is
present at index %d",
                            result);
    return 0;
}
```

Binary Search

The binary search algorithm does not work well with unsorted information. This means you should first use the sorting algorithm to clean up the data and store the information in an array. You should then write a function to find the element you are looking for in the array. A binary search algorithm breaks the array into segments and performs a linear search on the segment to find the required element. It is easier to perform a linear search, but a binary search is more efficient.

This algorithm will ignore the other elements in the array after it performs one comparison. Follow the steps given below to perform a binary search on the array elements:

1. Define the array and list the elements in the array. List the element you want to search for

2. Sort the elements in the array. Now, compare the target element with the middle element

3. If the element is the same, return the index or location of that element

4. If the target element is greater than the middle element, it will be present in the section to the right of the middle element. If it is lesser than the middle element, it will be present in the section to the left of the middle element

5. Perform the steps from 2 – 4 with the left or right section of the array

6. Otherwise, check the other half

7. End the search

Implementation

```
#include <stdio.h>
// This program is an example of a recursive
binary search function. It will return the
```

location of x in the given array arr[l..r]
if the element is present. Otherwise, it
returns the value -1

```c
int binarySearch(int arr[], int l, int r,
int x)
{
    if (r >= l) {
        int mid = l + (r - l) / 2;
        // If the element is the same as the
element in the middle of the array, then it
returns the index of the middle element
        if (arr[mid] == x)
            return mid;

        // If an element is smaller than the
middle element, then the element will only
be present in the left section of the array.
We will now perform a search on that section
        if (arr[mid] > x)
            return binarySearch(arr, l, mid
- 1, x);

        // Else the element can only be
present in the right section of the array
        return binarySearch(arr, mid + 1, r,
x);
    }

    // We reach here when element is not
present in the array itself
    return -1;
}
int main(void)
{
    int arr[] = { 2, 3, 4, 10, 40 };
    int n = sizeof(arr) / sizeof(arr[0]);
```

```
      int x = 10;
      int result = binarySearch(arr, 0, n - 1,
x);
      (result == -1) ? printf("Element is not
present in array")
                  : printf("Element is
present at index %d",
                        result);
      return 0;
}
```

Let us now look at how we can implement the binary search algorithm using the iterative and recursive methods. Before this, it is important to understand the time complexity of any binary search algorithm, especially to ensure you do not spend the machine's time unnecessarily on compiling. The formula to use is: $T(n) = T(n/2) + c$. To remove the recurrence in the code, use a recurrence or master tree method.

Recursive implementation

```
// To implement recursive Binary Search
using C++
#include <bits/stdc++.h>
using namespace std;

// In this code, we will use a recursive
binary search function. It returns the
location of the variable x in a given array
arr[l..r] is present.
// otherwise it will return the value -1
int binarySearch(int arr[], int l, int r,
int x)
{
    if (r >= l) {
```

```cpp
        int mid = l + (r - l) / 2;

        // If the element is present in the
middle of the array
        if (arr[mid] == x)
            return mid;

        // If element is smaller than mid,
then it indicates the element is present in
the left subarray
        if (arr[mid] > x)
            return binarySearch(arr, l, mid
- 1, x);

        // Else the element can only be
present in the other section of the array
        return binarySearch(arr, mid + 1, r,
x);
    }

    // If the element is not present in the
array, the compiler reaches this point
    return -1;
}

int main(void)
{
    int arr[] = { 2, 3, 4, 10, 40 };
    int x = 10;
    int n = sizeof(arr) / sizeof(arr[0]);
    int result = binarySearch(arr, 0, n - 1,
x);
    (result == -1) ? cout << "Element is not
present in array"
                   : cout << "Element is
present at index " << result;
```

```
        return 0;
}
```
The output of the code is: 'Element is present at index 3'

Iterative implementation

```cpp
// To implement recursive Binary Search
using C++
#include <bits/stdc++.h>
using namespace std;

// In this code, we will use a recursive
binary search function. It returns the
location of the variable x in a given array
arr[l..r] is present.
// otherwise it will return the value -1
int binarySearch(int arr[], int l, int r,
int x)
{
    while (l <= r) {
        int m = l + (r - l) / 2;

        // Check if x is present at mid
        if (arr[m] == x)
            return m;

        // If x greater, ignore left half of
the array
        if (arr[m] < x)
            l = m + 1;

        // If x is smaller, ignore right
half of the array
        else
            r = m - 1;
    }
```

```
    // If the compiler does not find the
element in the array, the compiler reaches
this stage
    return -1;
}

int main(void)
{
    int arr[] = { 2, 3, 4, 10, 40 };
    int x = 10;
    int n = sizeof(arr) / sizeof(arr[0]);
    int result = binarySearch(arr, 0, n - 1,
x);
    (result == -1) ? cout << "Element is not
present in array"
                    : cout << "Element is
present at index " << result;
    return 0;
}
```

The output of the code is: 'Element is present at index 3'

Jump Search

This algorithm is like the binary search algorithm. It looks for the element you want to find in the array. Bear in mind that, like the binary search algorithm, the jump search algorithm only works if the array is sorted. The objective of this algorithm is to look for the element from a smaller section of the array. This means the compiler skips some elements in the array to jump to another section in the algorithm.

Let us look at an example to understand this concept better. Let us assume you have created an array with 'n' elements in them. You can indicate to the compiler to jump ahead by a few steps. If you want to look for the search element in the array, you begin to look at the following indices a[0], a[m], a[2m], ... a[km]. The linear search will begin if the compiler finds the interval where the element may be present.

Consider the following array: (0, 1, 1, 2, 3, 5, 8, 13, 21, 34, 55, 89, 144, 233, 377, 610). There are 16 elements in this array. Now, let us indicate to the compiler to look for 55 in the array, and we will tell the compiler to break the code down into four subsections. This indicates the compiler will move by four elements every time.

Step 1: The compiler moves from the index 0 to 2.

Step 2: The compiler moves from 3 to 13.

Step 3: The compiler jumps from 21 to 89.

Step 4: The element in position 12 is larger than 55, so we go back to the start of the block.

Step 5: The linear search algorithm kicks in and looks for the index of the element.

Optimal Block Size

If you use the jump search algorithm, choose the right block size, so the compiler does not come across too many issues in the algorithm. In some cases, you may need to traverse through the entire list, but this is only dependent on where the element is and how well you optimize the code. Sometimes, you need to perform m-1 comparisons when the linear search algorithm kicks in. This is the worst-case scenario, and it means the number of jumps will be ((n/m) + m-1). The value of this function will be minimum if the value of the element 'm' is square root n. Therefore, $m = \sqrt{n}$ is the number of steps the compiler must run.

```cpp
// To implement Jump Search using C++
  #include <bits/stdc++.h>
using namespace std;

int jumpSearch(int arr[], int x, int n)
{
    // Finding block size to be jumped
    int step = sqrt(n);

    // Finding the block where element is
    // present (if it is present)
    int prev = 0;
    while (arr[min(step, n)-1] < x)
    {
        prev = step;
        step += sqrt(n);
        if (prev >= n)
            return -1;
    }

    // Doing a linear search for x in block
    // beginning with prev.
    while (arr[prev] < x)
    {
        prev++;
```

```cpp
        // If we reached next block or end
of
        // array, element is not present.
        if (prev == min(step, n))
            return -1;
    }
    // If element is found
    if (arr[prev] == x)
        return prev;

    return -1;
}

// Driver program to test function
int main()
{
    int arr[] = { 0, 1, 1, 2, 3, 5, 8, 13,
21,
                  34, 55, 89, 144, 233, 377,
610 };
    int x = 55;
    int n = sizeof(arr) / sizeof(arr[0]);

    // Find the index of 'x' using Jump
Search
    int index = jumpSearch(arr, x, n);

    // Print the index where 'x' is located
    count << "\nNumber " << x << " is at
index " << index;
    return 0;
}
```
The output of this code: Number 55 is at
index 10

The following points are to be kept in mind when you write an algorithm:

- You must sort the elements in the array before you use the algorithm

- The optimal length the compiler must traverse through is $\sqrt{n}$. Therefore, the time complexity of this algorithm is $O(\sqrt{n})$. This indicates the binary search and linear search algorithms are performed together to ensure the algorithm is not too complex

- The jump search algorithm is not as good as the binary search algorithm in terms of efficiency, but it is better than the binary search algorithm since the compiler only moves once through the array. If the binary search algorithm is too expensive in terms of memory and time, use the jump search algorithm instead

Sorting Algorithms

You can use different sorting algorithms to arrange a given list of elements or array based on the comparison operator used while defining the algorithm. This comparison operator will decide the order of the elements in the new data structure.

Sorting Terminology

Before we look at the different sorting algorithms you can use in programming, we will define some terms you must understand before you start using sorting algorithms.

External and Internal Sorting

The external sorting algorithm does not use a lot of space in the memory. The elements in the array are not loaded into the memory, and therefore, this sorting mechanism is often used to sort large volumes of data. Merge sort is an example of an external sorting algorithm, and we will look at this in further detail later in the book. Unlike the external sorting algorithm, an internal sorting algorithm uses a lot of space in the memory.

In-Place Sorting

If you only want to change a given input or reorder the elements in the input, you can use an in-place sorting algorithm. This algorithm will only sort the list of elements in the array by changing the order of the elements within the same list. For example, you can use the selection sort and insertion sort algorithms to sort a list of elements. Merge sort, and other sorting algorithms are not in-place sorting algorithms.

Stability

If you have multiple keys in the data set, you should consider the stability of the algorithm you want to use. For instance, remove duplicates from your list if you have some names in the algorithm you are using as keys. Therefore, it makes sense for you to sort the information in the data structure based on these keys.

What Is Stability?

When you have duplicate keys in a list, the sorting algorithm should ensure that these keys appear in the same order when you sort the output. Only when this happens is a sorting algorithm said to be stable. If you want to define this mathematically:

Let the array of elements be defined as A. We will define the strict weak ordering as '<' on the elements in the array. The sorting algorithm will then be stable if:

```
i<j and A(i) = A (j) implies C(i) < C(j)
```

Where C. denotes the sorting permutation, it means that the sorting algorithm will move the element at A(i) to C(i). In simple words, you can define the stability of a sorting algorithm based on the relative position of the variables in the algorithm.

Looking at Simple Arrays

If you have a list of elements where a single element is the key, the algorithm's stability will not be an issue. The stability of an algorithm will not be an issue even if the keys are all different.

Let us consider the following data set where we have the names of students against their sections.

```
(John, A)
(Betty, C)
(Jane, C)
(David, B)
(Erica, B)
```

If you instruct the algorithm to sort the data based on the name only, the resulting output will have a list that is not completely sorted.

```
(Betty, C)
(Erica, B)
(David, B)
(Jane,  C)
(John,  A)
```

So, in this instance, you may also need to sort the algorithm based on the section. If the sorting algorithm is not stable, you will get the following result:

```
(John,  A)
(David, B)
 (Erica, B)
 (Jane,  C)
 (Betty, C)
```

If you look at the output, you know that the data set is sorted based on the sections and not on the names. If you look at the order of the elements, you will see that the relativity in the sorting algorithm is lost. If you have a stable sorting algorithm, your output will be as follows:

```
(John,  A)
(David, B)
(Erica, B)
(Betty, C)
(Jane,  C)
```

If you look at the above output, you can see that the relative order is maintained between the tuples. It could be the case that the order is maintained even in an unstable sorting algorithm, but this is very unlikely.

Stable Sorting Algorithms

Some stable algorithms are:

1. Count Sort

2. Merge Sort

3. Insertion Sort

4. Bubble Sort

Sorting algorithms like insertion and merge sort the data based on the following parameters: The element A(i) will come before A(j) if A(i)<A(j) where i and j denote the indices. The relative order of the elements in the array is preserved since i<j. Like the count sort, other sorting algorithms maintain stability in the algorithm by sorting the data set in reverse order, so the elements have the same relative position. Radix sort, another stable sorting algorithm, depends on another sort performed where the only requirement is that the first sort should be stable.

Unstable Sorting Algorithms

Heapsort, quick sort, etc., are some unstable sort algorithms, but you can make these stable by looking at the relative position of the elements. You can make this change without compromising the performance of the algorithm.

Common Algorithms

Quick Sort

This algorithm uses the concept of the divide and conquer algorithm. It picks the elements in an array and divides them into segments. It then chooses an element from the array as a pivot and splits the array into segments based on the pivot. You can perform a quick sort using one of the following methods:

1. Choose the median of the elements as the pivot

2. Choose the last element in the array as the pivot

3. Choose any random element as the pivot

4. Choose the first element in the array as the pivot

The important part of this process is the partition or utility function. The objective of this function is used to sort the elements in an array based on a pivot. So, it will take the pivot, place that pivot in the middle and order the other elements around that pivot.

Implementation

```c
#include<stdio.h>
// We will now introduce a utility function
used to swap two elements in the array
void swap(int* a, int* b)
{
    int t = *a;
    *a = *b;
    *b = t;
}
```

/* This utility function uses the last element as the pivot and places the pivot element at its correct position in the sorted array. The function then places all smaller (smaller than pivot) to left of pivot and all the larger elements in the array to the right of pivot element */

```c
int partition (int arr[], int low, int high)
{
    int pivot = arr[high];    // pivot
    int i = (low - 1);  // Index of smaller
element

    for (int j = low; j <= high- 1; j++)
    {
        // If current element is smaller
than the pivot
        if (arr[j] < pivot)
        {
            i++;    // increment index of
smaller element
            swap(&arr[i], &arr[j]);
        }
    }
    swap(&arr[i + 1], &arr[high]);
    return (i + 1);
}

/* The main function that implements
QuickSort
 arr[] --> Array to be sorted,
  low  --> Starting index,
  high  --> Ending index */
void quickSort(int arr[], int low, int high)
{
    if (low < high)
```

```c
    {
        /* pi is partitioning index, arr[p]
is now
            at right place */
        int pi = partition(arr, low, high);

        // Separately sort elements before
        // partition and after partition
        quickSort(arr, low, pi - 1);
        quickSort(arr, pi + 1, high);
    }
}

/* Function to print an array */
void printArray(int arr[], int size)
{
    int i;
    for (i=0; i < size; i++)
        printf("%d ", arr[i]);
    printf("n");
}

// Driver program to test above functions
int main()
{
    int arr[] = {10, 7, 8, 9, 1, 5};
    int n = sizeof(arr)/sizeof(arr[0]);
    quickSort(arr, 0, n-1);
    printf("Sorted array: n");
    printArray(arr, n);
    return 0;
}
```

Understanding the Partition Algorithm

```
/* low  --> Starting index,  high  -->
Ending index */
quickSort(arr[], low, high)
{
    if (low < high)
    {
        /* pi is partitioning index, arr[pi]
is now
        at right place */
        pi = partition(arr, low, high);

        quickSort(arr, low, pi - 1);  //
Before pi
        quickSort(arr, pi + 1, high); //
After pi
    }
}
The pseudo code for the partition algorithm
is:
/* low  --> Starting index,  high  -->
Ending index */
quickSort(arr[], low, high)
{
    if (low < high)
    {
        /* pi is partitioning index, arr[pi]
is now
        at right place */
        pi = partition(arr, low, high);

        quickSort(arr, low, pi - 1);  //
Before pi
        quickSort(arr, pi + 1, high); //
After pi
    }
}
```

```
}
/* This function takes last element as
pivot, places
    the pivot element at its correct position
in sorted
    array, and places all smaller (smaller
than pivot)
    to left of pivot and all greater elements
to right
    of pivot */
partition (arr[], low, high)
{
    // pivot (Element to be placed at right
position)
    pivot = arr[high];

    i = (low - 1)   // Index of smaller
element

    for (j = low; j <= high- 1; j++)
    {
        // If current element is smaller
than the pivot
        if (arr[j] < pivot)
        {
            i++;      // increment index of
smaller element
            swap arr[i] and arr[j]
        }
    }
    swap arr[i + 1] and arr[high])
    return (i + 1)
}
```
Let us look at the illustration of this
function:
arr[] = {10, 80, 30, 90, 40, 50, 70}

```
Indexes:  0   1   2   3   4   5   6

low = 0, high =  6, pivot = arr[h] = 70
Initialize index of smaller element, i = -1

Traverse elements from j = low to high-1
j = 0 : Since arr[j] <= pivot, do i++ and
swap(arr[i], arr[j])
i = 0
arr[] = {10, 80, 30, 90, 40, 50, 70} // No
change as i and j
                                    // are
same

j = 1 : Since arr[j] > pivot, do nothing
// No change in i and arr[]

j = 2 : Since arr[j] <= pivot, do i++ and
swap(arr[i], arr[j])
i = 1
arr[] = {10, 30, 80, 90, 40, 50, 70} // We
swap 80 and 30

j = 3 : Since arr[j] > pivot, do nothing
// No change in i and arr[]

j = 4 : Since arr[j] <= pivot, do i++ and
swap(arr[i], arr[j])
i = 2
arr[] = {10, 30, 40, 90, 80, 50, 70} // 80
and 40 Swapped
j = 5 : Since arr[j] <= pivot, do i++ and
swap arr[i] with arr[j]
i = 3
arr[] = {10, 30, 40, 50, 80, 90, 70} // 90
and 50 Swapped
```

We come out of the loop because j is now
equal to high-1.
Finally we place pivot at correct position
by swapping
arr[i+1] and arr[high] (or pivot)
arr[] = {10, 30, 40, 50, 70, 90, 80} // 80
and 70 Swapped

Now 70 is at its correct place. All elements
smaller than
70 are before it, and all elements greater
than 70 are after
it.
Let us look at how to implement this
algorithm in C++:

```cpp
/* C++ implementation of QuickSort */
#include <bits/stdc++.h>
using namespace std;

// A utility function to swap two elements
void swap(int* a, int* b)
{
    int t = *a;
    *a = *b;
    *b = t;
}

/* This function takes last element as
pivot, places
the pivot element at its correct position in
sorted
array, and places all smaller (smaller than
pivot)
to left of pivot and all greater elements to
right
```

```
of pivot */
int partition (int arr[], int low, int high)
{
    int pivot = arr[high]; // pivot
    int i = (low - 1); // Index of smaller
element

    for (int j = low; j <= high - 1; j++)
    {
        // If current element is smaller
than the pivot
        if (arr[j] < pivot)
        {
            i++; // increment index of
smaller element
            swap(&arr[i], &arr[j]);
        }
    }
    swap(&arr[i + 1], &arr[high]);
    return (i + 1);
}

/* The main function that implements
QuickSort
arr[] --> Array to be sorted,
low --> Starting index,
high --> Ending index */
void quickSort(int arr[], int low, int high)
{
    if (low < high)
    {
        /* pi is partitioning index, arr[p]
is now
        at right place */
        int pi = partition(arr, low, high);
```

```
            // Separately sort elements before
            // partition and after partition
            quickSort(arr, low, pi - 1);
            quickSort(arr, pi + 1, high);
    }
}

/* Function to print an array */
void printArray(int arr[], int size)
{
    int i;
    for (i = 0; i < size; i++)
        cout << arr[i] << " ";
    cout << endl;
}

// Driver Code
int main()
{
    int arr[] = {10, 7, 8, 9, 1, 5};
    int n = sizeof(arr) / sizeof(arr[0]);
    quickSort(arr, 0, n - 1);
    cout << "Sorted array: \n";
    printArray(arr, n);
    return 0;
}
```

Selection Sort

The selection sort algorithm breaks the array into segments and sorts each segment by looking for the minimum element in the unsorted segment and moving it to the front of the array. The algorithm maintains two segments:

1. The sorted segment

2. The remaining part of the array, the algorithm should sort

The algorithm moves the minimum element from the unsorted segment to the sorted segment in each iteration.

Let us consider the following example:

We have an array array1[] = {10, 65, 40, 12, 22}. The objective is to find the minimum element in the above array and move it to the beginning of the array. Since the minimum element is at the start of the array, the array will not change.

```
array1[] = {10, 65, 40, 12, 22}
```

Now, the algorithm will look for the minimum element between the second and last element and move it to the smaller one to the beginning. The array will now look as follows:

```
array1[] = {10, 12, 65, 40, 22}
```

The algorithm will continue to break the array into segments, and the output will be:

```
array1[] = {10, 12, 22, 40, 65}
```

Implementation

```
#include<stdio.h>
int main(){
```

/* Using this program, the variables i and j are loop counters. The variable temp is used for swapping, and it holds the total number of elements in the array.

* The variable number[] is used to store all the input elements for the array, and the size of this array will change based on the necessity. */

```c
int i, j, count, temp, number[25];
printf("Number of elements: ");
scanf("%d",&count);
printf("Enter %d elements: ", count);
// Loop to get the elements stored in
array
for(i=0;i<count;i++)
    scanf("%d",&number[i]);
// Logic of selection sort algorithm
for(i=0;i<count;i++){
    for(j=i+1;j<count;j++){
        if(number[i]>number[j]){
            temp=number[i];
            number[i]=number[j];
            number[j]=temp;
        }
    }
}
printf("Sorted elements: ");
for(i=0;i<count;i++)
    printf(" %d",number[i]);
return 0;
}
```

Bubble Sort

The bubble sort algorithm is a very simple and easy-to-use sorting algorithm. It compares adjacent elements and sorts the elements based on the ascending order. If the position of the elements does not need to change, the elements are sorted. The process followed using this sorting algorithm is stated below:

1. Define the array and its elements

2. Use a statement to calculate the length of the array and store the number in the variable 'n'

3. The following steps should be performed for the elements in the array:

4. Use the loop covering the elements starting with the index (i) = 1 and ending at n and another loop for every element starting with index (j) = n and ending at i+1, perform the following steps:

   a. If A[j] < A[j-1]

   b. Move the element at the index Array [j] to the position Array [j-1]

5. End the algorithm

Consider the following example:

First Pass:

        (5 1 4 2 8) -> (1 5 4 2 8)

In this step, the algorithm will compare the elements in the array and swap the numbers 1 and 5.

            (1 5 4 2 8) -> (1 4 5 2 8)

In this step, the numbers 4 and 5 are swapped since the number 5 is greater than 4.

```
( 1 4 5 2 8 ) -> ( 1 4 2 5 8 )
```

In this step, the numbers 5 and 2 are swapped.

```
( 1 4 2 5 8 ) -> ( 1 4 2 5 8 )
```

In the last step, the elements are ordered, so no more swapping is necessary.

Second Pass:

```
( 1 4 2 5 8 ) -> ( 1 4 2 5 8 )
( 1 4 2 5 8 ) -> ( 1 2 4 5 8 )
```

In this step, the numbers 4 and 2 are swapped since the number 4 is greater than 2.

```
( 1 2 4 5 8 ) -> ( 1 2 4 5 8 )
( 1 2 4 5 8 ) -> ( 1 2 4 5 8 )
```

Since the compiler cannot determine the array is sorted, it will run the code again.

Third Pass:

```
( 1 2 4 5 8 ) -> ( 1 2 4 5 8 )
( 1 2 4 5 8 ) -> ( 1 2 4 5 8 )
( 1 2 4 5 8 ) -> ( 1 2 4 5 8 )
( 1 2 4 5 8 ) -> ( 1 2 4 5 8 )
```

Consider the following implementations of the bubble sort algorithm:

```cpp
// Implementation of the algorithm on C++
#include <bits/stdc++.h>
using namespace std;
```

```cpp
void swap(int *xp, int *yp)
{
    int temp = *xp;
    *xp = *yp;
    *yp = temp;
}

// A function to implement bubble sort
void bubbleSort(int arr[], int n)
{
    int i, j;
    for (i = 0; i < n-1; i++)

    // Last i elements are already in place
    for (j = 0; j < n-i-1; j++)
        if (arr[j] > arr[j+1])
            swap(&arr[j], &arr[j+1]);
}

/* Function to print an array */
void printArray(int arr[], int size)
{
    int i;
    for (i = 0; i < size; i++)
        cout << arr[i] << " ";
    cout << endl;
}

// Driver code
int main()
{
    int arr[] = {64, 34, 25, 12, 22, 11,
90};
    int n = sizeof(arr)/sizeof(arr[0]);
    bubbleSort(arr, n);
```

```
        cout<<"Sorted array: \n";
        printArray(arr, n);
        return 0;
    }
```

The output of this code is:

Sorted array:

```
11 12 22 25 34 64 90
```

Insertion Sort

The insertion sort algorithm is very simple to use. The algorithm works the same way as the process you use to sort playing cards. The algorithm follows the process below:

1. Create an array with any number of elements, and define it using the following method: array1 [n]

2. Use a loop function and run it from the first element in the array until the end of the array. Now, choose the element and insert the element into the sequence

3. Add a condition so the element is included in the array based on its array size

4. End the algorithm

Let us consider the following example:

Define an array Array1[5] and add variables to that array: Array1[] = {12, 11, 13, 5, 6}. Now, add a loop to the array and begin the function from the first element. The loop should move until the last element in the array. Since the second number is less than the first number, the algorithm will move it before 11.

$$Array1[] = \{11, 12, 13, 5, 6\}$$

The loop now moves to the third element in the array, but the array will change since the elements before the third element are smaller than the third element.

$$Array1[] = \{11, 12, 13, 5, 6\}$$

Now, the loop moves to the fourth element in the array. It compares the other elements in the array with the previous numbers in the array. Since the number is smaller than all the other numbers, it will move to the front.

$$Array1[] = \{5, 11, 12, 13, 6\}$$

The loop finally moves to the last number in the array, and since this number is less than the three numbers before it but greater than the first number, it will move to the second position.

$$Array1[] = \{5, 6, 11, 12, 13\}$$

Implementation

```
#include <math.h>
#include <stdio.h>
   /* Function to sort an array using
insertion sort*/
void insertionSort(int arr[], int n)
{
    int i, key, j;
    for (i = 1; i < n; i++) {
        key = arr[i];
```

```c
        j = i - 1;
        /* Move elements of arr[0..i-1],
that are
        greater than key, to one position
ahead
        of their current position */
        while (j >= 0 && arr[j] > key) {
            arr[j + 1] = arr[j];
            j = j - 1;
        }
        arr[j + 1] = key;
    }
}
    // A utility function to print an array of
size n
void printArray(int arr[], int n)
{
    int i;
    for (i = 0; i < n; i++)
        printf("%d ", arr[i]);
    printf("\n");
}
    /* Driver program to test insertion sort
*/
int main()
{
    int arr[] = { 12, 11, 13, 5, 6 };
    int n = sizeof(arr) / sizeof(arr[0]);
    insertionSort(arr, n);
    printArray(arr, n);
    return 0;
}
```

Merge Sort

Like the quick sort algorithm, the merge sort algorithm works is also a divide and conquer algorithm. In this sorting algorithm, the input array is broken into two halves. The sorting algorithm will be called to sort the elements in each of the halves and then merge the array into one array. You can use the merge function to merge the two halves. You must enter the following parameters when you perform a merge sort algorithm:

1. The input array, along with its elements

2. First sorted half

3. Second sorted half

Using the merge sort algorithm, you can merge the two arrays. Let us first look at how the algorithm functions before we look at the implementation.

1. Define the array and add the elements to it

2. Divide the array into halves, and sort the elements in each half

3. Use the merge function to combine the sorted arrays

4. End the algorithm

Implementation

// Using this code, we will merge two subarrays of the array arr[]. The first subarray is arr[l..m], and the second is arr[m+1..r]

```
void merge(int arr[], int l, int m, int r)
{
    int i, j, k;
```

```
     int n1 = m - 1 + 1;
     int n2 =  r - m;

     /* create temp arrays */
     int L[n1], R[n2];

     /* Copy data to temp arrays L[] and R[]
*/
     for (i = 0; i < n1; i++)
         L[i] = arr[l + i];
     for (j = 0; j < n2; j++)
         R[j] = arr[m + 1+ j];

     /* Merge the temp arrays back into
arr[l..r]*/
     i = 0; // Initial index of first
subarray
     j = 0; // Initial index of second
subarray
     k = l; // Initial index of merged
subarray
     while (i < n1 && j < n2)
     {
         if (L[i] <= R[j])
         {
             arr[k] = L[i];
             i++;
         }
         else
         {
             arr[k] = R[j];
             j++;
         }
         k++;
     }
```

```
    /* Copy the remaining elements of L[],
if there
        are any */
    while (i < n1)
    {
        arr[k] = L[i];
        i++;
        k++;
    }

    /* Copy the remaining elements of R[],
if there
        are any */
    while (j < n2)
    {
        arr[k] = R[j];
        j++;
        k++;
    }
}

/* l is for left index and r is right index
of the
    sub-array of arr to be sorted */
void mergeSort(int arr[], int l, int r)
{
    if (l < r)
    {
        // Same as (l+r)/2, but avoids
overflow for
        // large l and h
        int m = l+(r-l)/2;

        // Sort first and second halves
        mergeSort(arr, l, m);
        mergeSort(arr, m+1, r);
```

```c
        merge(arr, l, m, r);
    }
}


/* UTILITY FUNCTIONS */
/* Function to print an array */
void printArray(int A[], int size)
{
    int i;
    for (i=0; i < size; i++)
        printf("%d ", A[i]);
    printf("\n");
}


/* Driver program to test above functions */
int main()
{
    int arr[] = {12, 11, 13, 5, 6, 7};
    int arr_size =
sizeof(arr)/sizeof(arr[0]);

    printf("Given array is \n");
    printArray(arr, arr_size);

    mergeSort(arr, 0, arr_size - 1);

    printf("\nSorted array is \n");
    printArray(arr, arr_size);
    return 0;
}
```

Chapter Eleven

Loop Control and Decision Making

As mentioned earlier, most algorithms use loops and decision-making statements. Therefore, it is important to understand how to run these algorithms in any programming language. Any programming language sequentially executes code. This means the first statement is executed before the compiler moves to the next one. You can, however, control this using loops and conditional statements. These functions allow you to perform complex operations on data.

Decision Making

This is a key piece of programming, and a programmer needs to know how to use decision-making statements to perform certain functions. The structures of decision-making statements include at least one condition that needs evaluating and testing by the program. It also has one or more statements the compiler must execute depending on the value of the condition. You may also include other statements to execute if the condition is false. The following are the decision-making statements in most programming languages:

?: Operator

We already touched on this earlier. The?: is a conditional operator used instead of an if...else statement, and its format looks something like:

State1? State2 : State3 ;

State1, State2, and State3 are all expressions – do note the use of the colon and its placement.

To work out what the value of the entire expression is, State1 is evaluated first:

If State1 has a value of True, the value of State2 will then be the value of the entire expression

If State1 evaluates to false, then State3 will be evaluated, and the value of State3 will be the value of the whole expression.

If Statement

The if statement is the most common decision-making statement used in programming. The condition has a Boolean expression and one or more statements in the body.

If Else Statement

This statement may be succeeded by an else statement, which is optional, which will execute should the Boolean expression evaluate false

Nested if

If you want to test many conditions, use a nested if statement since you can include multiple if statements and one else statement.

Switch Statement

The statement for use when you want to test a variable for equality against a list of given values

Loop Statements

If you want to execute statements numerous times in some lines of code, use loops. Most programming languages have three common loops:

1. For loop

2. While loop

3. Do While loop

For Loop

A for loop executes a statement numerous times depending on the condition stated in the parameters. The loop variable controls the number of times the loop runs. The syntax of this loop is:

```
for (initialization; condition; update)
{
      Body;
}
```

In the for loop, the loop variable is initialized in the function's parameters, and the value is either increased or decreased within the loop's body. The condition in the function above will result in a Boolean output – either true or false, and it determines the number of times the loop runs for. If the condition returns false, the loop will break, and the statements after the loop are executed. If the condition does not break, the loop continues to run indefinitely.

Consider the following example of a for loop where we want to print numbers 0 – 10:

```
for (int i = 0; i <= 10; i++)
{
Console.Write(i + " ");
}
```

You can use the loop to perform complicated functions. For example, you can calculate the power (m) of a number (n).

```
Console.Write("n = ");
int n = int.Parse(Console.ReadLine());
Console.Write("m = ");
int m = int.Parse(Console.ReadLine());
decimal result = 1;
for (int i = 0; i < m; i++)
{
result *= n;
}
Console.WriteLine("n^m = " + result);
```

In the above code, we calculate the power of the number within the loop's body. The condition we have set it against is the power (m). For loops can also have two variables defined and initialized within the condition.

```
for (int small=1, large=10; small<large;
small++, large--)
{
Console.WriteLine(small + " " + large);
}
```

While Loop

Using the while loop, you can repeat one or more statements in the body of the loop depending on the condition. The condition is tested before the loop body is executed.

The syntax of the loop is as follows:

```
while (condition)
{
      Body;
}
```

Consider the example below where we want to print the numbers 0 – 9 on the output window.

```
// Initializing the counter variable
int count = 0;
// Setting the loop with the required
condition
while (count <= 9)
{
// Printing the variable on the output
screen
Console.WriteLine("Number : " + count);
// Incremental operator
counter++;
}
```

The code will give out the following result:

```
Number: 0
Number: 1
Number: 2
Number: 3
Number: 4
Number: 5
Number: 6
Number: 7
Number: 8
Number: 9
```

Let us now look at how to calculate the sum of numbers 1 – 10.

```
int count = 0;
int sum = 0;
while (count <= 10)
{
sum=sum+count;
count++;
}
Console.WriteLine("The sum is" + sum);
```

You can do this in different ways depending on whether you want to use loops or not. We can also use the while loop to work on other mathematical calculations. The program below checks whether a number entered is a prime number or not.

```
Console.Write("Enter a positive number: ");
int num = int.Parse(Console.ReadLine());
int divider = 2; //stores the value of the
potential divisor
int maxDivider = (int)Math.Sqrt(num);
bool prime = true;
```

```
while (prime && (divider <= maxDivider))
{
if (num % divider == 0)
{
prime = false;
}
divider++;
}
Console.WriteLine("Prime? " + prime);
```

Do While Loop

The do…while loop is like the while loop except the loop body is executed before the condition is tested. This means the loop will execute once, even if the condition you have entered is false.

The syntax of the loop is as follows:

```
do
{
        Body;
} while (condition);
```

Once the statements in the body are run, the condition is checked. If the condition is true, then the loop runs again. This function is repeated till the condition is false. The body of the loop is executed at least once since the condition is checked only after the body is executed.

In the example below, we will calculate the factorial of a number.

```
using System;
using System.Numerics;
class Factorial
{
```

```
static void Main()
{
Console.Write("n = ");
int n = int.Parse(Console.ReadLine());
BigInteger factorial = 1;
do
{
factorial *= n;
n--;
} while (n > 0);
Console.WriteLine("n! = " + factorial);
}
}
```

If you run the program now, you can get the factorial of any number of your choosing.

Loop Control Statements

Loop control statements are used to change the normal sequence of execution. When the execution leaves its scope, i.e., it finishes what it set out to do, all the objects that were automatically created in the scope are then destroyed.

The following control statements are supported in most programming languages:

Break Statement

This operator can be used to break out of a loop. There are times when we may write an incorrect code, and the loop will run indefinitely. At such times, the break operator comes in handy since it will automatically bring you out of the loop. This statement can only be written inside the loop if you wish to terminate the iteration from taking place. The code after the break statement is not executed. The following example will show you the code used to calculate the factorial of a number.

```
int n = int.Parse(Console.ReadLine());
// "decimal" is the biggest data type that
can hold integer values
decimal factorial = 1;
// Perform an "infinite loop"
while (true)
{
if (n<=1)
{
    break;
}
factorial *= n;
n--;
}
Console.WriteLine("n! = " + factorial);
```

We have initialized a variable called factorial to read variables from 1 – n in the console. Since the condition is true, this creates an endless loop. Here the break statement will stop the loop from functioning when the value of n is less than or equal to 1. The loop will continue to run if the condition in the if statement does not hold true.

foreach loop

The foreach loop is an extension of the for loop in some programming languages, such as C, C++, and C#, but is a well-known loop. It is also used by PHP and VB programmers. This loop iterates and performs operations on all elements of an array or list.

It will operate on all the variables even if the list or array is not indexed. The syntax of the loop is as follows:

```
foreach (type variable in the collection)
{
        Body;
}
```

A foreach loop is like the for loop, but most programmers prefer this type of loop since it saves writing a code to go over all the elements in the list. Consider the following example to see how a foreach loop works:

```
int[] numbers = { 2, 3, 5, 7, 11, 13, 17, 19
};
foreach (int i in numbers)
{
Console.Write(" " + i);
}
Console.WriteLine();
string[] towns = { "London", "Paris",
"Milan", "New York" };
foreach (string town in towns)
{
Console.Write(" " + town);
}
```

In the example above, we created an array and then printed those numbers on the output screen using a foreach loop. Similarly, an array of strings is created, which are then printed onto the output window.

Nested Loops

As the name suggests, a nested loop has multiple loops within the main loop. The syntax is as follows:

```
for (initialization, verification, update)
{
for (initialization, verification, update)
{
     Body;
}
}
```

If the condition holds true in the main loop, the statements within the main loop are executed. Before you write a code with nested loops, it is important to write down the algorithm. You must determine how you want to organize the loops. Let us assume you want to print the numbers in the following format:

```
1
1 2
1 2 3
1 2 3 ...... n
```

You need two loops. The outer loop looks at the number of lines being executed and the inner loop looks at the elements within each line. The code has been given in the last chapter.

Continue Statement

The continue statement makes the loop skip the rest of the loop body and test the condition again before iterating over the sequence again. The following example describes the function of the statement.

```
int n = int.Parse(Console.ReadLine());
int sum = 0;
for (int i = 1; i <= n; i += 2)
{
if (i % 8 == 0)
{
continue;
}
sum += i;
}
Console.WriteLine("sum = " + sum);
```

In the above program, we calculate the sum of the integers not divisible by 8. The loop will run until it reaches a number that cannot be divided by 8.

Chapter Twelve

Introduction to Data Structures

Most programming languages allow you to use data structures, such as lists and arrays, and we have briefly looked at what these mean in the eighth chapter. In this chapter, we will look at how you can look at different methods you can use to define and use a data structure.

You will also learn how to use these data structures to define numerous variables or combine different elements, either input or output variables, across the entire program. A structure, however, allows you to combine different variables and data types. You can use a structure to define or represent records. Let us assume you want to arrange the bookshelf in your library. We will see how you can use a data structure to track different attributes of every book. For this example, we will look at the following attributes:

1. Book ID
2. Book title
3. Genre
4. Author

The Struct Statement

Before you define any data structure, it is important to use the struct statement to create that structure in the program. Bear in mind the struct statement works only in C and C++ languages. However, other programming languages use a different statement. You can also define the number of elements or members in the code.

Use the following syntax to define the structure in your code:

```
struct [structure tag] {
    member definition;
    member definition;
    ...
    member definition;
} [one or more structure variables];
```

There is no necessity to use the structure tag when you use the struct statement. Use the variable definition method to describe every member you want to use in the structure. If you are unsure how to describe the data, learn how to avoid making mistakes. For instance, you can use the method int i to define an integer variable. The section before the semicolon in the struct syntax is also optional. It is best to keep this in the program since you define the variables you want to use in the structure. Continuing with the example above, we will define the book structure using the following lines of code.

```
struct Books {
    int book_id;
    char book_title[50];
    char genre[50];
    char author[100];
} book;
```

144

Accessing Structure Members

It is easy to access data structure members using a full stop. This full stop is known as the member access operator. It is used as a break or period between the data structure members and the names of variables. Ensure to enter the variable name you want to access. You can define the variable of the entire structure using the struct keyword. Consider the following lines of code to understand how you can use structures. We will be continuing the example mentioned at the start of the chapter.

```
#include <iostream>
#include <cstring>
 using namespace std;
 struct Books {
    int book_id;
    char book_title[60];
    char genre[60];
    char author[40];
};
 int main() {
```

struct Books Book1; // *Using this statement, you can declare the first variable called Book1 in the data structure.*

struct Books Book2; // *Using this statement, you can declare the first variable called Book2 in the data structure.*

// *The next lines of code will instruct the compiler on how to add details to the first variable*

```
Book1.book_id = 1001;
strcpy( Book1.book_title, "Eragon");
```

```
    strcpy( Book1.genre, " Fantasy");
    strcpy( Book1.author, "Christopher
Paolini");
    // The next lines add data to the second
variable
    Book2.book_id = 1002;
    strcpy( Book2.book_title, "Eldest");
    strcpy( Book2.genre, "Fantasy");
    strcpy( Book2.author, "Christopher
Paolini");
```

// We will use the next lines of code to print the details of the first
and second variables in the data structure

```
    cout << "Book 1 id: " << Book1.book_id
<<endl;
    cout << "Book 1 title: " <<
Book1.book_title <<endl;
    cout << "Book 1 genre: " << Book1.genre
<<endl;
    cout << "Book 1 author: " << Book1.author
<<endl;
    cout << "Book 2 id: " << Book2.book_id
<<endl;
    cout << "Book 2 title: " <<
Book2.book_title <<endl;
    cout << "Book 2 genre: " << Book2.genre
<<endl;
    cout << "Book 2 author: " << Book2.author
<<endl;
    return 0;
}
```

Output:

The code above will give you the following output:

```
Book 1 id: 1001
Book 1 title: Eragon
Book 1 genre: Fantasy
Book 1 author: Christopher Paolini
Book 2 id: 1002
Book 2 title: Eldest
Book 2 genre: Fantasy
Book 2 author: Christopher Paolini
```

Using Structures as Arguments

A data structure can also be called as an argument in a function. This works in the same way you would pass any variable or pointer as a parameter in the function. To do this, you must only access the variables the way we did in the above example.

```
#include <iostream>
#include <cstring>
 using namespace std;
 struct Books {
   int book_id;
   char book_title[60];
   char genre[60];
   char author[40];
};
 int main() {
```

struct Books Book1; // *Using this statement, you can declare the first variable called Book1 in the data structure.*

struct Books Book2; // *Using this statement, you can declare the first variable called Book2 in the data structure.*

// *The next lines of code will instruct the compiler on how to add details to the first variable*

```
Book1.book_id = 1001;
strcpy( Book1.book_title, "Eragon");
strcpy( Book1.genre, " Fantasy");
strcpy( Book1.author, "Christopher
Paolini");
```

// *The next lines add data to the second variable*

```
Book2.book_id = 1002;
strcpy( Book2.book_title, "Eldest");
strcpy( Book2.genre, "Fantasy");
strcpy( Book2.author, "Christopher
Paolini");
```

// *Let us now look at how you can specify the details of the second variable*

```
Book2.book_id = 130000;
strcpy( Book2.book_title, "Harry Potter
and the Chamber of Secrets");
strcpy( Book2.genre, "Fiction");
strcpy( Book2.author, "JK Rowling");
```

// *The next statements are to print the details of the first and second variables in the structure*

```
printBook( Book1 );
printBook( Book2 );
return 0;
}
void printBook(struct Books book ) {
```

```
    cout << "Book id: " << book.book_id
<<endl;
    cout << "Book title: " << book.book_title
<<endl;
    cout << "Book genre: " << book.genre
<<endl;
    cout << "Book author: " <<
book.author<<endl;
}
```

Output:

When you compile the code written above, you receive the following output:

```
Book 1 id: 120000
Book 1 title: Harry Potter and the
Philosopher's Stone
Book 1 genre: Fiction
Book 1 author: JK Rowling
Book 2 id: 130000
Book 2 title: Harry Potter and the Chamber
of Secrets
Book 2 genre: Fiction
Book 2 author: JK Rowling
```

Using Pointers in Structures

You can also refer to structures using pointers, and you can use a pointer similar to how you would define a pointer for regular variables.

```
struct Books *struct_pointer;
```

When you use the above statement, you can use the pointer variable defined to store the address of the variables in the structure.

```
struct_pointer = &Book1;
```

You can also use a pointer to access one or members of the structure. To do this, you need to use the -> operator:

```
struct_pointer->title;
```

Let us rewrite the example above to indicate a member or the entire structure using a pointer.

```
#include <iostream>
#include <cstring>
 using namespace std;
void printBook( struct Books *book );
struct Books {
    int book_id;
    char book_title[50];
    char genre[50];
    char author[100];
};
 int main() {
```

struct Books Book1; // *This is where you declare the variable Book1 in the Book structure*

struct Books Book2; // *This is where you declare the variable Book2 in the Book structure*

// *Let us now look at how you can specify the details of the first variable*

```
    Book1.book_id = 1001;
    strcpy( Book1.book_title, "Eragon");
    strcpy( Book1.genre, "Fantasy");
    strcpy( Book1.author, "Christopher
Paolini");
```

// *Let us now look at how you can specify the details of the second variable*

```
    Book2.book_id = 1002;
    strcpy( Book2.book_title, "Eldest");
    strcpy( Book2.genre, "Fantasy");
    strcpy( Book2.author, "Christopher
Paolini");
```

// *The next statements are to print the details of the first and second variables in the structure*

```
    printBook( Book1 );
    printBook( Book2 );
    return 0;
}
```

// We will now use a function to accept a structure pointer as its parameter.

```
void printBook( struct Books *book ) {
    cout << "Book id: " << book->book_id
<<endl;
    cout << "Book title: " << book-
>book_title <<endl;
    cout << "Book genre: " << book-
>genre<<endl;
    cout << "Book author: " << book->author
<<endl;
```

```
}
```

When you write the above code, you obtain the following output:

```
Book id: 1001
Book title: Eragon
Book genre: Fantasy
Book author: Christopher Paolini
Book id: 1002
Book title: Eldest
Book genre: Fantasy
Book author: Christopher Paolini
```

Typedef Keyword

If you cannot define the data structure easily using the above methods, use an alias structure to define the structure. Consider the following example:

```
typedef struct {
    int book_id;
    char book_title[50];
    char genre[50];
    char author[100];
} Books;
```

It is easier to use this process to define the structure since you define the variables used in the structure without using the struct keyword.

```
Books Book1, Book2;
```

Bear in mind a typedef key is not required to define any data structure. You can use it to define any regular variable, as well.

```
typedef long int *pint32;
pint32 x, y, z;
```

The above lines of code show the compiler points to the x, y, and z variables.

Chapter Thirteen

Comments and Formatting

In this chapter, we will look at some points with respect to writing comments and formatting code. While your algorithm is the base of the code, it is important to describe every important step in the algorithm when you write the code. This is the only way it becomes easier for people to read and understand the code. Add comments to the code and determine how you want to explain the comments. As a developer, you must read the code regularly and ensure it is readable and understandable. So, stick to the formatting and indentation of your code.

Comments

It is important to understand how to write comments effectively. Most people wonder if they should add a lot of comments to explain every line of code. The issue with comments is that you often forget to update them. You may want to change the code, but it is possible you may ignore the comments. This would mean the comments reflect the older code.

A difficult thing to do is educate a programmer on writing comments in the code. The moment you change the code, you also need to change the comments. You should never forget about updating comments since this could lead to issues in the functioning of the code. You must look at the comments as documentation. Maintain these comments since it is the only way to explain what your code does. Ensure you add comments to express exactly what is happening in the code.

Features of Good Comments

Some comments are useful since they will add some value to the code.

Clarification and Intention

Comments are the best way to explain your intent behind writing the code. This does not mean you should use comments to explain every line of code. Your code should do it. It is important to explain what it is that you wanted to do in the code. In some situations, you cannot express the intention behind writing the code. For this reason, you need to add some comments to explain why you took a specific action. Some methods may have been used to deal with external library issues, or maybe you had to incorporate odd requests. It is important to explain these sections in better detail no matter what it is.

```
// Code to check if the input variables are
valid
function is_valid($first_name, $last_name,
$age) {
    if (
```

```php
        !ctype_alpha($_POST['first_name'])
OR
        !ctype_alpha($_POST['last_name']) OR
        !ctype_digit($_POST['age'])
        ) {
        return false;
    }
    return true;
}
switch(animal) {
    case 1:
        cat();
        // falls through
    case 2:
        dog();
        break;
}
```

Informative and Legal

It is important to add comments to the code for many reasons. Some laws also require comments to be written to explain what each line in the code means. The code can always be written under specific license terms. Therefore, it is important to specify the code. In such cases, it is important to specify the code. Therefore, you need to add some comments to specify the operation of the code.

You can use comments to point to specific URLs in the document if you need to. This is the only way to explain how the code is written. Do not have more than 200 lines of comments to explain this information. Some comments may add value to the code, while others do not. For example, you can give information about the method and the value that is returned by the method. Be careful before you place a comment. You can also remove the comments if needed, but it is important to ensure you explain exactly what the code is supposed to do.

Features of Bad Comments

Adding Unnecessary Comments

Ensure you only add comments to the code when you should. Do not add comments only because you are expected to. This will affect the look of the code. If you add comments with no necessity, you end up having too much unnecessary information in your code. You may end up with many comments irrelevant to the actual code. This will make it hard for you to read the code or even understand it. So, avoid adding unnecessary comments.

Code Explanation

You may have some code that is hard for you to explain, and it is probably because you cannot understand the code. This does not mean you should use comments as a way to solve the issue. Ensure that you rewrite the code and rename the elements in the code, like functions, variables, data structures, and other objects, so the reader understands what action you are performing. In most cases, you extract the method using mindful names. These names make it easier for the reader to understand how the code uses the method.

Redundant

If you name the method or field accurately, you do not have to comment against that code line. You can describe the function, field, or method using comments. You do not have to describe the scope of the variable. For example, methods named "SendEmail" do not require any additional comments. The name is self-explanatory. This is especially true when the variable is called. The method will send the email as the output. Another example can be "storeValueForCurrentOrder." This variable means the current order value is stored in the variable. Do not write a comment to explain the same thing. The comment does not add any value to the code.

Position Markers

You mustn't use any position markers in the code. You cannot add ////// to the code just so you can find a specific part of the code.

Journal

It is important to document why you change certain sections of the code. You must journal these changes since this is the only way to give another person an idea why the code is changing. It is also the only way for you to determine why the code changed. Some programming languages allow you to track the changes made to the code. Now, you no longer need comments to track changes but can activate the tracking mechanism in the language.

Mandated, Noise and Misleading

Unfortunately, not many people explain what they plan on doing with the code. It is only for this reason you may add comments against inconsequential statements. Some programmers may add lines of code to say they are printing a variable or sending an email. These comments are useless since they do not explain what was done to perform those operations. Sometimes you may have errors

158

in your code, and if you have such bad comments, you cannot identify where the issue actually is. You may only identify the error once you read through the entire code, which makes the comments written in the code useless.

Ugly Code

People often use comments in the code where the code is often hard to read or understand, i.e. ugly code. The comments are often used to fix the lines of code. Do not make the code beautiful by adding comments. If the code is ugly, refactor the code and update it. Write it in a way to make it easier for you to see what is exactly being done in the code.

Formatting

Formatting and Coding Style

Bear in mind to stick to one style of formatting only when you write code. If you work with a team, ensure the team knows exactly what style to stick to. Never waste precious time formatting the code. There are different ways to format the code, and you will find some examples across the book. The internet also has multiple formats you can stick to. Never change the formatting styles in the middle of writing the code. If you have multiple people in the team, understand how each of them likes to code and format the text. This will help you remain open to newer coding standards and allow you to accept those standards. Ensure you also write the code well.

Functions

Functions are dependent on each other, and they may inherit some functionalities or values from other modules and functions in the code. You must have the child functions in the parent function. It is easier to do this only if you can easily read the code you have written. You will no longer have to navigate through the code to find the child functions in the code.

Indentation

It is very important to indent any code you write. Stick to the same standard when you write code. Do this even if you need to break the rules. When you stick to the indentation rules, it becomes easier for you to identify the variables and other important aspects of the code. With new tools and IDEs, it is easy to follow the same indentation standards everywhere in the code.

Code Affinity

Ensure the code written for the same purpose, including the variables, functions, and objects, are maintained in one section of the code. Do not write the code in such a way that you must scroll through the entire file a million times to find the required functionality.

Chapter Fourteen

Debugging

D o not spend too much time trying to debug the code and identify issues in it. Be prepared for errors to exist in the code. Put in a lot of effort to debug the code. Follow the steps given below to prepare yourself for the arduous task. This will make it easier for you to assess the code and make changes needed to ensure it compiles without errors.

Understand the Algorithm and Design

It is important to understand the algorithm fully before you write any code. Otherwise, you will do something you never wanted to in the first place. You cannot test the module if you do not understand the design since you have no idea what the objective of the module is. If you are using another's code as a reference, review the algorithm, design, and comments to understand the objective of the code. If you do not know how the algorithm functions, you cannot develop effective test cases, and this is true when you use data structures in your code. This means you cannot determine if the algorithm works as expected.

161

Check the Correctness of the Code

Different methods can debug code and determine if the written information is correct and the compiler runs without throwing errors.

Peer Reviews

It is best to have another person, someone well-versedin writing code, to assess and examine the code you have written. If you want the review to be effective, you must ensure the peer has the required information and knowledge to check the code. It is important to give the peer the code with the comments so he knows exactly what to expect in the code.

If you want to make it easier for the peer, you can explain the code to them and tell them how the algorithm functions. If the reviewer disagrees or does not understand some parts of the implementation, you need to discuss it with him until you both reach an agreement. The objective of the peer should be to detect the errors in the code. It becomes easier to correct them if identified correctly.

You can identify these issues yourself when you proof the code. Having said that, it is useful if you have someone from the outside looking at the code and identifying some blind spots in the code. Peer reviews will take time, so ensure you restrict the reviews to only those sections of code you want to be assessed and not the entire code.

Code Tracing

You can detect errors in code easily by tracing the execution of different functions and modules in the code. It is especially important to do this when calls are made to the function or module in different parts of the program. As the programmer, you must trace how the functions and modules work. If you want this process to be effective, you should trace the modules and functions by assuming that other functions and procedures in the code work accurately. When performing code tracing, you must deal with different layers or levels of inheritance and abstraction. Bear in mind that you cannot find all errors through tracing. This process, however, improves your understanding of the algorithm used.

Proof of Correctness

The best way to identify any error in the code is to examine the algorithm used and use different methods to validate the correctness of the algorithm. For example, if you know the preconditions, terminating conditions, invariants, and postconditions in any loop statement used, you can perform simple checks in the code. Ask the following questions to determine the correctness of the code:

1. If the compiler has entered the loop without throwing any error, does it mean the invariant used is accurate?

2. If the statements in the loop body do not throw an error, does it mean the loop has worked well and will terminate without any error?

3. If the loop is nearing the end, does it mean the compiler will move towards the postcondition?

These questions may not help you determine if there are errors in the code, but it gives you an understanding of the algorithm being used better.

Anticipate Errors

It is not unfortunate to have errors in the code since there is a possibility you may use incorrect pointers and variables in the code. You may also forget to call or use certain functions and parameters in the code. We also make mistakes when it comes to tracing the code, and peer reviews may not catch all the errors in the code. You must be prepared for these errors in the code and use the error handling techniques we discussed earlier in the book.

Conclusion

Thank you for purchasing the book. If you have just started programming, it is important to learn how algorithms work and use those algorithms to write code. This book has all the information you need about structuring your programs. The book introduces you to the concept of algorithms and how they can be used to write high-performing code. It also introduces the concept of sorting and searching algorithms.

Use the information and examples in the book to improve your understanding of algorithms. Practice and learn to write code so it performs better than any other code you have written before.

I hope you have gathered the information you are looking for.

Resources

Advantages and disadvantages of algorithm and flowchart - Computersciencementor | Hardware, Software, Networking and programming. (n.d.). Computersciencementor.com. https://computersciencementor.com/advantages-and-disadvantages-of-algorithm-and-flowchart/

Bubble sort in C | Programming Simplified. (2020). Programmingsimplified.com. https://www.programmingsimplified.com/c/source-code/c-program-bubble-sort

DAA - Space Complexities - Tutorialspoint. (2019). Tutorialspoint.com. https://www.tutorialspoint.com/design_and_analysis_of_algor ithms/design_and_analysis_of_algorithms_space_complexitie s.htm

Includehelp. (2017). Includehelp.com. https://www.includehelp.com/data-structure-tutorial/algorithm-and-its-types.aspx

GeeksforGeeks | A computer science portal for geeks. (2019). GeeksforGeeks. https://www.geeksforgeeks.org/

Selection Sort Program in C. (2015, February 11).
    Beginnersbook.com.
    https://beginnersbook.com/2015/02/selection-sort-program-in-c/

Types of Algorithms | Learn The Top 6 Important Types of
    Algorithms. (2019, May 10). EDUCBA.
    https://www.educba.com/types-of-algorithms/

What are the Advantages and Disadvantages of Algorithm. (2018,
    August 23). Vedantu.com.
    https://www.vedantu.com/question-answer/what-are-the-advantages-and-disadvantages-of-algorithm-5b7ea609e4b084fdbbfacd20

www.ingramcontent.com/pod-product-compliance
Lightning Source LLC
Chambersburg PA
CBHW071414210326
41597CB00020B/3506